ASSESSING MANAGEMENT PEOPLE:
A Practical Guide

ASSESSING MANAGEMENT PEOPLE

A Practical Guide

J.A. DUKES

ROUTLEDGE

First published in 1988 by
Routledge
11 New Fetter Lane, London EC4P 4EE
Reprinted 1990

Printed in Great Britain
by Billings & Sons Limited, Worcester.

British Library Cataloguing in Publication Data

Dukes, J.A.
Assessing management people.
1. Managers. Assessment
I. Title
658.4′07125

ISBN 0-415-00823-9 Pbk

Contents

Foreword

Jim Dukes says that he aims to be readable, relevant and right. I can assess whether he has achieved the first two and he clearly has.

The combination of his long experience of assessment and his sabbatical year devoted to assessment should also ensure that he is right. There is a further characteristic of this book: it is enjoyable.

Anyone in management has to assess others. Doing so is not easy, whether it is to fill a vacancy, to assess present performance or future potential. Readers of Jim Dukes' book will be helped to have a better understanding of what they are doing and to avoid some of the traps for the unwary and the arrogant.

Rosemary Stewart
Templeton College

Preface

This is a practical book for those engaged in the assessment of managers and other high level staff. In it, I have set out to describe the procedures that assessors should follow and to treat the difficulties they are likely to encounter with understanding. In so doing, I have aimed to be readable, relevant and right.

Reading about assessment over the years, I have read a lot that was obscure and imprecise — accompanied by varying claims to profundity in unstated extenuation — but nothing that could not be better said in plain language. In consequence I have aimed at the simplest English compatible with technical accuracy. Nevertheless, a book which aims to cover such a complex topic in a comprehensive way inevitably makes some demands on its readers. A newcomer to systematic assessment who does not find reading easy is earnestly requested to discard the assumption that a book is to be read once only. For such, a light first reading is recommended. Further reading after some experience will offer increased dividends, when the subject-matter will be more familiar. There is a summary at the end of each chapter. Some may find it helpful to read this before the chapter itself. With the same aim of being helpful to the reader, I have discussed some complex concepts which require more thought, separately from the main text, in the appendices.

Throughout, sex-neutral terms are used where they are available. Unfortunately, however, English has no third person singular pronoun of this sort, and I have not attempted to avoid the use of 'he' and 'his' where such contrivance would make for awkward expression. I have solved a lesser problem by using 'candidate' throughout to describe the person being assessed.

For the second aim — relevance and the fact that this book came to be written — I must record my thanks to the many hundred assessors I have worked with. The book is the result of a great many queries and requests for advice. Responding to these, it became clear that, as far as high-level selection is concerned, much had been written about techniques but little on how to interpret the results and even less on how to use such evidence to reach a well-founded decision. My aim is to fill this vital gap. I have written about obtaining evidence and weighing it and consequently I have written about methods with uncompromising attention to the user's needs, leaving the discussion of technicalities with others.

My third aim — that of being right — is something that the reader should be able to take for granted. It is, however, necessary to nod in the direction of our academic critics who complain that much of what we do has not been scientifically established. The assertion is valid but fails in understanding of the real world. A manager who waited for scientific certainty would accomplish nothing. What is needed in assessment is the ability to take rational decisions on the best available evidence, without needing to believe that one is infallible or in possession of universal truths, but rather with the humility that includes a willingness to learn continually from experience. This book is based on the experience of many people who have not only been very widely engaged in assessment, but have also been at pains to follow up and validate their results. In consequence, I have been able to write with the confidence that the reader's own experience will increasingly confirm the value of the advice given here.

Acknowledgements

It is impossible to make adequate acknowledgements to all the colleagues I have worked with and who have told me of their organisations, techniques and problems over the last two decades. But some names stand out. The influence of Dr Edgar Anstey and Ken Murray will be obvious to the many who have also learned from them. I have also learned much from daily discussions with Jaimie Dodd — now transfigured as The Reverend J.H.B. Dodd — who also made many useful comments on this book. I am in the debt of Dr Charles Bethell-Fox and Brian Venner who read chapters for me and that of Joan Swindells who patiently read the book in its entirety. I owe a special debt to Teddy Morgan for his help in arranging the sabbatical during which most of this book was written. To my father, J.A. Dukes Senior, I am indebted for a lifetime of trenchant comment on the working life of an entrepreneur. An almost equally long-standing debt is to Dr E.N.Williams, who first interested me in the problems of assessment and has never ceased to teach me the difficult art of writing by both precept and example.

I am grateful to the President and fellows of Templeton College (Oxford Centre for Management Studies) with whom I spent an idyllic year thinking and writing about assessment. Among the fellows I owe a special debt to Dan Gowler, Janine Napahiet and Dr Rosemary Stewart. Further thanks are due to the students of the College who paid me the great compliment of treating me as one of themselves and supplied me with many vivid and helpful accounts of their job-hunting experiences. Among them, Femi Oguntukun and Vincent Poon (Tak On) were especially helpful.

My greatest debt, without doubt, is to the thousands of candidates who have undergone my assessments. I hope that they found the experience as stimulating as I did.

Finally, having acknowledged the generous and indispensable help of others, I must emphasise that responsibility for everything written here is mine alone.

J.A. Dukes

For Leena

1
The Business of Assessment

Why assessment?

Any organisation is only as good as the people who work in it, so that efficiency depends vitally on appointing the right staff and using their talents in the right way. This means that managers have to assess people for a number of purposes — for recruitment, for promotion, for assignment to new jobs, to compile routine staff reports or simply to make the best day-to-day use of their abilities.

Such assessments are seldom limited to what people can do here and now. Much more often they involve what they might do in future — if given a job, if given greater responsibility, or if moved to an unfamiliar area of work. Assessment therefore usually involves prediction and, for some of the assessed, the time-scale involved can be that of an entire career. Assessors can be looking at a school-leaver or a new graduate and deciding whether he can make a useful contribution to their organisation for something like 40 years.

Unsurprisingly, assessment is an error prone activity and there can be few who would not wish that they could perform it more efficiently. This is not to be either defensive or apologetic. Decisions have to be taken, and as with other management decisions, the evidence available is seldom complete and may indeed be seriously defective. In such a situation, even the most skilled and experienced judges can make serious mistakes. For those without training and experience the procedure is much more hazardous.

Further, many organisations set high standards of fairness for individual applicants, making the whole task of appraisal more difficult. It may generally be easy enough to fill a job with someone who can do it, to select a competent candidate or to promote a promising person. It is a great deal more difficult to leave the unsuccessful with the impression that their case has been fully and fairly considered. Some organisations make no pretence of doing this, and many cannot afford to do so. Many however, accept this as an essential requirement, not only on grounds of equity, but also for reasons of efficiency. Such a requirement means that assessment must be thorough and rigorous.

Sources of error

Judgements of others are often mistaken and for a number of reasons — some obvious, some not. In the first place, it must be observed that our ignorance of people is in some areas profound. In a novel situation people show unsuspected strengths and weaknesses. Some grow into a bigger job, expand and flourish. Some pass a threshold and manifestly fail to cope. In this area, in particular, human judgement is likely to remain fallible.

On the other hand, anyone with any experience of working life is equipped with a considerable experience of other people and the way they behave. We all have considerable resources to draw upon. At the same time, however, our experience of other people is affected by the circumstances in which we interact with them. They may be behaving formally in a situation governed by clear social rules such as a committee meeting. They may be responding to strong signals we are putting out — directing, encouraging, praising, reprimanding, negotiating, arguing, persuading and so on. In these situations neutral observation is impossible, and impressions gained from such experiences may be seriously misleading.

Less obvious sources of error are the numerous legends that exist in this area. The following is from *The Times* of Saturday 4 February 1978. It describes the recruiting techniques of the first head of the British Secret Service, Sir Mansfield Cumming or 'C' as he called himself.

> Cumming employed novel methods in recruiting the young Richard Hannay figures who entered his unpaid service. During their interview he would roll up his trouser leg, pluck a match from the folds of his jacket, strike it on his wooden leg and light up his foul-smelling pipe. Unless the would-be

spy prattled on regardless about his rowing career at Oxford, he was out.

One cannot share the obvious approval with which the writer invests this account. In highly concentrated form it embodies some of the basic fallacies that bedevil this difficult activity.

These are:

1. For any job, people must be made of 'the right stuff'.
2. Each of us has some concealed 'real self'.
3. This 'real self' can be uncovered by some one infallible test.
4. There are people of piercing insight who can instantly identify the 'real self' behind everyday appearances.

These beliefs are clearly mutually supporting. More to the practical point they are seldom explicitly recognised for what they are, and, being implicitly accepted, are so much the more powerful in their working. Since they are fallacious, this is a serious matter, and they need to be examined in some detail.

1. The belief that some people are made of 'the right stuff' (and that some correspondingly are not) pervades human history. In saga, the obvious requirement was physical courage. Nowadays, the requirements have filled out a little. The Victorians — as exemplified by their headmasters — added some stern moral requirements. And Tom Wolfe's popular book *The Right Stuff* shows how the idea was applied in the selection of American astronauts

Whatever its history and origins, the idea is demonstrably absurd. To succeed in any job but the simplest requires a mixture and, generally a balance, of different qualities. There can be very few cases where success or failure depends entirely on one characteristic.

2. The idea of the concealed 'real self' might be of more recent origin. At least Greek legend and Nordic saga described people in uncomplicated terms. In the present day, however, people make strong distinctions between appearance and reality.

Here many things are true. First appearances may be misleading, or initial judgements may turn out to be false. People can dissimulate and give convincing expression to opinions they do not hold. Further, many qualities are not apparent to immediate observation — drive, reliability and staying power, for example, and these are more important than an immediately observable social manner. All these points are valid, but they do not justify the declaration that some human characteristics are real and some are not.

Sometimes assessors recommend a candidate after a difficult appraisal based on confused or uncertain evidence. If the candidate turns out well, it is natural to say that the assessors had discerned the 'real person' hidden behind the confusing appearances. In fact, many things may have happened. The assessors may have made a lucky guess. The candidate may have been taken in hand by a capable mentor. The assessors may have discerned that the candidate had the vital qualities for success despite less appealing ones. To say then that they identified the 'real person' hidden behind appearances is simply to obscure what they did and how they did it in an unprofitable way.

3. Sometimes, under stress, shock, or unexpected or challenging conditions, people may behave in ways that surprise the observer, and sometimes themselves. In these circumstances, an observer may learn something new and valuable about them. He may decide that he has learned something that does not fit with the personality that he has credited them with. He might have found a clue to a lot he had not suspected. He might have seen a feature that is inconsistent with what he knows about a person. What he has not done is uncover a real and hidden person consistent with that one incident. Because a normally placid person once loses his temper, it makes no sense to claim that he really is a bad-tempered person.

4. Some people are better judges than others. As in other human activities, however, there are no supermen, and no one has the gift of immediately evaluating other people in an infallible way. Such people belong to legend and imaginative fiction where characteristically they have 'piercing eyes' or 'a shrewd gaze'. Such descriptions suggest some highly developed vision which can penetrate secret places of the human personality. There is no such thing. Accurate assessment can never be carried out quickly and effortlessly. In essence, an assessor is solving a problem, and the activity resembles other sorts of problem solving in many ways. It requires the careful collection of evidence, a conscious effort to fill gaps and the testing of possible solutions to find the one most acceptable. Collecting evidence may involve special testing procedures and, since the activity consists essentially of one human being judging another, it requires a degree of caution and detachment which a purely intellectual problem does not.

The process

The process of assessment may be seen at its fullest and most explicit in selection — deciding to take a previously unknown person into the organisation. For this reason and to avoid repetition and verbal clumsiness, it is convenient to write mainly in terms of selection, rather than promotion and assignment. This facilitates a comprehensive coverage of the ground. Those concerned with assessment for those other purposes will find it easy to take what they need.

Selection itself is an activity for which widely different resources are available. Some large organisations use a five- or six-day procedure of great thoroughness. Such thoroughness looks expensive and many organisations use a simpler procedure. In some the assessment might be limited to an interview of half an hour. In all cases, however, the problems and the approaches to an answer are the same. The shorter the procedure, however, the more assessors have to be selective in deciding which areas require examination and what must be taken for granted in assessing an individual candidate.

The outstanding all-rounder that every assessor hopes to meet is, by definition, in short supply. He is also in great demand and only an organisation that pays unusually well or has a highly attractive image can hope to fill its needs with such people. But the reality for most organisations will include careful scrutiny of a fair number of borderline cases.

Assessors therefore have to be prepared to meet some difficult candidates. There are cases where highly developed qualities which would be of great use to the organisation have to be balanced against marked weaknesses. There are people who are complex and difficult to appraise. Some people — particularly some valuable kinds of specialist — who are bad at being interviewed, so that the job calls for great patience and unusual understanding.

A book which aims to be comprehensive by covering such situations may have the unfortunate side-effect of making the whole business seem impossibly complicated or hazard-strewn. This is certainly not so. In many cases, the process of assessment is straightforward and the result clear-cut. But the present objective is to cover the whole range of questions that will be met. And in doing so my aim has been not only to instruct but also to help the reader make the best possible use of his own judgement and experience.

Like any other kind of management decision making,

assessment has its moments of stress, perplexity and tedium. It also has moments of humour and, more important, moments of great satisfaction from finding the right person for the job. For those interested in their fellow humans the process can be consistently stimulating and enjoyable. And the exercise of the skills of assessment can be highly rewarding in themselves.

Summary

Successful appraisal is a demanding activity, systematic in approach and explicit in reasoning. There are no supermen in this activity, any more than there are in any management activity. Everyone is equipped with a degree of knowledge of his fellow humans, but to use this effectively assessors have to possess a degree of self-awareness, and to know of the ways in which experience can mislead.

2
The Theoretical Background

People are theorists

Since this is a practical book for practical people, a chapter with such a heading might seem superfluous if not perverse. But the fact is that people — even the most down to earth — are incorrigible theorists.

This is a point that has been investigated intensively in the last three decades. This book is not the place to describe such research in detail, but the reader may find it profitable to reflect on the fact that we are constantly finding ourselves in situations which we have not previously experienced. We do not analyse these afresh every time we come across them. When we drive round a corner for the first time we do not examine the view carefully to see if the road continues or comes to an abrupt and unannounced end. Life would be impossible if lived on these terms. Very early in life people build up expectations of what their future experience will be like. Because the world is a fairly consistent place and, without being aware of doing so, we put a lot of effort in childhood into developing these expectations and testing their application, we can as adults cope efficiently with a wide range of novel situations.

This fact is important, because there was a time when scientific enquiry — or even common honesty — seemed to require us to approach any appraisal with a completely open mind. There are many who would unquestioningly accept this as the necessary approach today. It was always recognised that this was an arduous undertaking, but modern research has demonstrated convincingly that it is an impossible one. The simple unavoidable fact is that we interpret our present experience by means of a very large number of preconceived ideas developed from our previous experiences. It does not matter whether one refers to them as preconceived ideas, constructs, stereotypes, images or templates. What is important is to realise that these are an inescapable part of our experience, that some are useful and some can be seriously misleading. What is even more important is to distinguish the former from the latter and a large part of this book is devoted to such an objective. This chapter deals with some of the higher level problems which confront the reflective assessor. They are discussed in turn.

You never know what someone else is thinking

This is largely true in what it says and seriously misleading in what it implies. What is certainly true is that, if someone states 'I am thinking about Queen Victoria' and he is in fact thinking about his next summer holiday, one has no way of knowing that this is so. It is an inescapable feature of life that a person may conceal his thoughts and, if he wishes, give a totally false account of them.

This is not universally true, however. If someone on one day discusses the merits of rival cars, then on another day the advantages and disadvantages of different sorts of credit, and on a third whether it is better to buy a new or a second-hand car, and on a later day the merits of various garages, we might not be impressed by his denial that he was thinking of buying another car. But the general principle that thoughts are private and known only to the thinker unless he reveals them is unchallengeable.

But if this principle is taken to imply that there is a fatal flaw in any attempt at appraisal it is seriously misleading. We want to know many things about people. We want to know how clever they are — and in any but the simplest appraisal they cannot pretend to be cleverer than they are. We wish to know how well a candidate can communicate and he could not utter a few halting sentences and then claim to be an impressive speaker. We want to know if they can cope with stress, persevere with a taxing task and respond energetically to a challenge. In all these situations we may decide to discount any statement that the candidate makes about himself. Certainly, if there is any conflict between such a personal statement and what we observe in his long-term behaviour, then we would not give weight to his personal claims.

This is not to claim that there are no problems. People may conceal feelings of embarrassment, anger or distaste. They may plausibly claim a liking for a job or person they detest. And the cases of Burgess, Maclean and Philby demonstrate that, in extreme cases, people may succeed in persistent deceptions for half a lifetime. But there is an important gap between infallibility and a high degree of competence. And the fact that assessors can never achieve the former does not mean that they cannot achieve the latter.

People know themselves best

The discussion so far has been in terms of dishonesty or at least misrepresentation. In fact, deliberate and systematic dishonesty is fairly uncommon. On the whole people do not want jobs for which they are unsuitable, and, having done their best by their own lights, are reasonably content to leave the judgement to their assessors.

Further in many contexts sincerity is of no importance. Or rather it is irrelevant to the point under consideration. People may sincerely believe themselves to be hard working, reliable or energetic, and be nothing of the kind. They sometimes state that they are lazy or mean, when they are energetic or generous. Nearly everybody thinks they are shyer than in fact they are.

The belief that people know themselves best, dignified in philosophy as the 'Theory of Privileged Access', has very little to commend it — especially when one examines it for truth. The simple fact is that understanding oneself is a different sort of activity from understanding others, and in general it seems to be more difficult. For this there seem to be two mutually supporting reasons. Firstly, our own behaviour is not displayed to us in the same way as other people's is. Secondly, our self-esteem is involved when we are assessing ourselves in a way that that it is not when we assess others.

It may be for these reasons that people can often be puzzled by themselves, when others are not. While it is a natural reaction for a perplexed assessor to put weight on the apparent sincerity of a candidate's answers, this tendency must be controlled. Apparent conviction may be irrelevant. A stumbling and hesitant answer may be the more useful and, indeed, the more sincere.

What is insight?

This is a deeply puzzling question. Clearly, insight is a desirable quality, and the more an assessor has the better. But how can one improve such a mysterious faculty? The fiction in which some amazing feats of the required kind are performed merely adds to the puzzling legend. As already noted, novelists tend to speak of keen gazes and piercing eyes, treating insight as though it were the name of some extra visual faculty — some sort of psychic projection.

Any such suggestion is clearly nonsense. And it is worrying nonsense at that. We would all like to improve our insight. But when it is described in these terms we are set a mysterious and impossible task. There is no conceivable method that we can follow.

In practice, we have simply to recognise that the term is a metaphor — comprehensible as such but still unhelpful. Having recognised this, we can go on to ask how one human being can understand another.

There are, in essence, two views on this. One holds that we understand other people only through our own experience. The other holds that we can acquire insights from others. On the first view, we recognise that the experience of someone else resembles our own. This is not to say that they are identical or that we can relive their experiences in any literal sense. We cannot experience their ambitions, achievements, disappointments, hopes and fears. More to the immediate point, we cannot share their experience in the other chair as we interview them. What we can do is to recognise significant similarities between these as they describe them, and our own experiences of these states.

Significance, of course, is a different thing for the parent, the lover, the creditor and the teacher. For our purposes, we are working with a notion of significance that concerns the prediction of behaviour. We want to know how people will cope with a job, how they will see and exploit opportunities, deal with disappointments and so on.

This view of insight emphasises the need for assessors with a wide experience of life. The more a person has experienced, the more he is equipped to make sense of the experience of others. This is not only a matter of theory; it is supported by everyday observation.

In the second view of our understanding of others, it is asserted that we learn theories or generalisations which explain their behaviour. There are certainly large numbers of such generalisations around both in folk wisdom and psychological theories. They are of varying usefulness. Red-haired people are said to be quick-tempered, physical scientists are not very good at social relations, mathematicians tend to be interested in music, chess is a useful training for military tactics and the like. And psychologists have their theories about introverts and extroverts, the way in which basic tendencies to be seen in the child are modified in the adult, and so on.

These two views — adapting our own experience and learning theories — are often presented as rivals. Common sense might be taken to support the view that they are complementary. Nobody's experience is wide enough to cover every case — we need to learn from the experience of others. On the other hand theories are not enough on their own. It is a notorious fact that psychology students have been shown to be less insightful than arts students. This is not necessarily a criticism of psychologists or their theories. It merely supports the view that to apply theories with understanding people need an experience of life, the entities the theories refer to, in order to see how they fit in. It therefore seems a safe conclusion that insight is something that is acquired from both kinds of source.

Taking a broad view of what has been established, the following points seem to be valid:

1. Some people are much better at understanding people than others. There is a range of ability in this respect as there is in others.
2. No one understands everybody else. People have different ranges of understanding which overlap those of others.
3. The more other people resemble oneself and the more their experiences resemble one's own the easier it is to understand them.
4. People's untutored understanding of others varies. It can be improved.

This last point brings us to a central question. How? Part of the answer lies in terms of improving techniques — particularly those of interviewing. Part lies in an assessor extending the range of his ideas.

Such an extension develops naturally from our experience of working life. We learn about the realities of work, but we learn about the real satisfactions as well as less enjoyable parts. We observe some people doing well and some not so well and produce explanations for what we see. We note that some people do well at a particular sort of job or situation. On the other hand, there is a recognisable tendency for people's range of acquaintances to narrow as they grow older. It is easier to meet others with the same background and interests. Assessors may therefore find themselves less well equipped to understand young candidates or those with an unusual background, from a foreign culture or with some strange personal attitudes.

Further, assessors may not learn much from colleagues. Americans are more open than the British, who tend to be impersonal in their working contacts. We can sometimes learn more about a candidate in a brief interview than we learn about a colleague in several years. We do learn in this way from candidates. Sometimes we get an insight into a novel view of life and an experience widely removed from our own. Enlightenment to this degree is unusual, but from most candidates we can extend our range to some degree.

What assessors can do is learn from other people's insights. Biographies, historical accounts and imaginative fiction, books, films and plays of the right kind offer many explanations of human conduct, motives and attitudes. A discriminating reading of these can do much to extend the range of an assessor's perceptions and understanding.

There have been investigations designed to find out what sort of person has the widest and most reliable insights. The results have been contradictory and puzzling. Often the investigations have been limited to short-term judgements. It has been announced that the best judges are timid people or authoritarian people. This seems unhelpful in the present context. There is not much point in finding which personality characteristics show some correlation with good judgement of people. What we want to know is what people in general need if they are to understand others.

The requirements that suggest themselves are firstly an interest in understanding people and a willingness to work at developing it. Secondly, an open mind is necessary — a willingness to understand and respond sympathetically to other points of view and other ways of life. Allied to these qualities one needs a corresponding range of concepts to structure what one sees efficiently and this necessarily involves verbal skills — possessing and being able to employ a comprehensive vocabulary to describe human conduct.

Natural interest in others varies widely, but those who are willing to work at it can improve their understanding significantly. Those who do this successfully are free of restricting preconceptions and rigid theories of human behaviour.

Objectivity

The need for assessors to be objective is unchallengeable. This being so it might seem that there is nothing to be discussed. However, there are dangers in over-simple notions of what objectivity requires. Such notions generally take the following form. An assessor must adopt an attitude of complete detachment. His own views, feelings and attitudes are recognised as irrelevant. He simply ignores them and conducts his appraisal in completely intellectual terms. As an aim this is beyond criticism. As a description of the way in which objectivity can be achieved it is hopeless. And for this there are two main reasons — one psychological and one logical. One does not have to be a profound or experienced psychologist to realise that our attitudes are formed by many childhood and later experiences of which we are unaware. To suggest that we can simply distance ourselves from these experiences when we do not know what they are is to make a rather implausible claim.

This might be less implausible if detachment were a logical possibility. It is not. It is impossible to make completely intellectual judgements because not all judgements are completely intellectual. To claim that they are would be to claim that there are no differences in kind between the statements that 'snow is white', 'stones are hard', 'feathers are light' on the one hand, and 'Democracy is the best form of government', 'Property is theft' and 'Crime deserves punishment' on the other. While much intellectual effort has been devoted to the attempt to demonstrate that the differences are illusory, it is obvious to most people that the difference is real and important. One set of statements is of matters of fact; the other of values. There is a clear and fundamental distinction between the two. This is necessarily an abstract one — there are transitional cases. 'Gas is expensive', 'You must drive on the left in the UK', and 'John is hard working' do not fall easily into either category. But on the face of it there is no difficulty in analysing such statements in terms of facts and values.

The simple point about values is that they are not purely intellectual entities. They reflect human attitudes. If one adopted a purely intellectual attitude one could not distinguish between the candidate dedicated to the abolition of private property and the one who accepted it as a fact of life. And clearly one wants to be able to make this kind of distinction. We therefore seem to have arrived at a position of some difficulty. Objectivity is desirable but impossible. This, however, is to overstate a good case. It must be a valid requirement that anyone wishing to work in an organisation should be willing to accept the basic values of that organisation. No one expects the Church to employ atheists and no commercial undertaking would be expected to employ someone dedicated to the overthrow of capitalism. It is not necessary to insist that these values are completely intellectual in their foundation to make this valid and obvious point.

Nothing said so far should be taken as a denial of the need for objective appraisal. What is rather being asserted is the need to understand what objectivity involves. More generally, since complete detachment is psychologically impossible, a better notion of what objectivity involves is needed. An example may help at this point. We tend to exaggerate the importance of qualities in which we regard ourselves as exceptionally strong or weak. A person who tends to think of himself as lazy will have a natural tendency to regard energy as the outstandingly important requirement for the job. Someone who thinks he has a very strong sense of humour (a rather large proportion of the population) will emphasise the necessity for a sense of humour in the candidate.

These are distortions of judgement and must be avoided. The immediate question is as to how this is to be done. The immediate answer is by self-knowledge. If one knows that one has a natural tendency to overestimate energy or humour one can correct this tendency. If one is naturally inclined to take it for granted that people will be likeable, one can take care to look more carefully at this point.

In short, the picture of the assessor as completely detached recognises an important principle but is naive in its application. We should not think in terms of an impossible kind of detachment. To do so would be self-defeating. We should rather think in terms of self-knowledge, being aware of our natural predilections and compensating for them to form a balanced judgement.

Summary

This chapter has dealt with some large-scale background issues. It has been pointed out that the notion of a completely open mind is not tenable. It has placed the privacy of thinking in a practical context and shown that this is not a major hindrance to the successful assessment of others. The nature of insight and means of improving it have been discussed. The important notion of objectivity and the distinction between facts and values have also been discussed.

3
The Practical Approach

There are some 60,000 words which can be used to describe human personality. Given the ways in which such descriptions might be combined to describe an individual, an assessor is faced with a near-infinite number of possibilities.

Clearly in this situation an assessor has to impose order on primitive chaos — to structure his observations in some way. In devising a structure for assessment, the first principle must be relevance. The assessor must ask which qualities are vital for the job, which are important and which are rather beside the point. There are many fascinating, witty and interesting things he can say about people and he can enjoy saying them. Stern self-discipline is necessary, however, and he must concentrate on the essentials. To do this systematically and economically he needs two aids — a job description and a specification for the person who can do it.

The person for the job

In the days when supermarkets and self-service stores were unheard of, British needs were largely supplied by small shops which employed errand boys on bicycles to deliver provisions to the customer's door. It was then quite common to see notices in shop windows saying 'smart lad wanted'. It has to be observed that many organisations have not got a lot further in defining their requirements for managers.

This is not to be purely critical. There are many difficulties in this area, some of which have yet to be recognised and dealt with by professionals. And research findings have been inconclusive or puzzling in a number of ways. The reader willing to try a simple experiment can easily gain an insight into some of these.

This is to try asking people what they need in a factory storeman (or a postman, security guard or messenger). An intelligent man? — certainly. Initiative? — indispensable. Physically fit? — essential. Energetic? — the organisation is built on such people. Before long, you have a specification for a senior manager of sprightly constitution; certainly not someone who will want to work for a storeman's wage.

This is clearly an impossible specification. To avoid this sort of situation it is necessary to take a close look at what such storemen actually do. They are mainly valued for the speed with which they can supply requests for stores from the shop-floor. In order to be able to make a quick response to such requests, the storeman cannot get deeply engaged in other tasks. There is a limit to the amount of tidying up that can be done and this means that, of necessity, the storeman must spend a lot of time simply waiting for orders. An intelligent man would soon be bored. An energetic man would soon find limits to the amount of tidying up he could do and become similarly bored. Initiative would be wasted and the lack of opportunity for its exercise would lead to frustration. A number of studies have in fact established that a high and unwelcome turnover in staff has been due to recruiting over-qualified people in this sort of way.

This example illustrates a principle which is firmly embedded in modern occupational psychology. Before making out a person specification it is necessary to complete a job description. Or, more succinctly, before deciding what sort of person you want, you must take a close and realistic look at the job he is going to do.

However, there are complications. The approach works well with lower grade jobs like those of filing clerk or lathe operator, but less well for that of manager. There are a number of reasons for this.

The first and most obvious, is that anyone joining an organisation at this level is unlikely to expect to remain in one job for his working life. A machinist or secretary will generally expect to work at the same level for their working lives, but managers and professionals expect either to be promoted within the organisation or move to a better job outside it.

The recruiting organisation needs to be clear about this situation. Is there a career within the organisation for the person recruited? Or will he have to move if he wishes to better himself? (And it will need to bear in mind that a good candidate may so move at an inconvenient time for the organisation. A less satisfactory one may cling to the job, providing continuity but at a lower or unacceptable level of efficiency.) There are circumstances — when the candidate is near retiring age, for example — where the person recruited might be expected to stay in the job for the rest of his working life, but these are not common. More commonly, a job specification is necessary when filling a particular post from within the organisation.

Otherwise, when the job is filled by recruitment, the specification for the person to fill it cannot be derived purely from the description of that first job. Normally something more than immediate competence will be required and, in particular, the capacity to grow into more demanding jobs.

But there is another complication which distinguishes the job of the manager from that of the lathe operator. To fill the latter's job it is enough to observe what present operators are doing and describe this for use by the recruiters. With managers the situation is different. For a managerial job there is a core requirement — things that must be done — and an area of discretion, where an individual will have choices over what he will do. He may concentrate on particular aspects of his predecessor's activities. He may hand over or push some aspects on to his colleagues. He may decide that some activities can be safely neglected or abandoned. He may open up new areas or persuade others that he should take some over from them or he may simply push his way into doing so. For these reasons, a job description which simply describes what the existing holder does will be inadequate, if not seriously misleading.

This means that a job description at this level must be in rather general terms, with a greater weight on objectives than on closely described activities. The following demonstrates the kind of description which should be adapted to the requirements of the individual organisation, when a particular post is to be filled.

Job Title: Chief Scientist XYZ Food Company

Responsible to: Managing Director

Responsible for: Four qualified (graduate) chemists and biologists and two laboratory assistants.

Objectives: To maintain quality control of firm's production in regard to health requirements.

To make recommendations for improved handling of products when necessary.

To improve cost-effectiveness of testing methods. (This

section would be expanded in more detail for the individual firm.)

Salary and benefits:

These headings would cover most appointments, but it might be necessary to add another — 'activities' — to some.

This it has already been observed is for use with an appointment to a particular job and for assigning an existing manager to a job within the organisation, but would be of little use where a career with the organisation is possible. Here, when people attempt what they may call a job description, they in fact most often produce a list of activities. This is more easily done for the job of specialist than for that of a general manager. The following description for an Operational Research Scientist, would suit most organisations.

'An OR scientist's working life may be largely described in terms of projects — management problems which may be very large in scale. In junior grades he will probably play an auxiliary role, helping with part of a project. At a higher level he will be running his own. At senior levels he will be supervising and setting up projects.

At the most senior levels, however, the job will be less concerned with project work but more with the identification of areas where OR may be usefully applied. In a general sense, this will involve educating management in the potential and actual use of the OR approach. And there will be traces of these activities at the junior levels.

At the same time senior scientists are engaged in staff supervision, reporting and the like and some regard to the qualities needed for these activities is also necessary.

But given that projects are the essential form of OR work, the job requirements are best related in terms of the development of a project. While every project is different, all can be described in terms of six stages. This is an abstract classification and two or more stages may overlap, but an OR scientist in control of his work will keep track of the degree to which he has accomplished each.'

(The six stages and the qualities most required at each would then be described).

But there is a further difficulty in describing the work of a general manager. The argument so far may have read as common sense. But another vital point may seem less so. This is that any analysis must take place within a certain framework of ideas. It might seem an obvious requirement that anyone should approach such a task with an open mind, but this is in fact impossible. To draw up such a description, the investigator has to abstract from what he observes. To decide what is significant and label it correctly he must be equipped with an appropriate conceptual structure.

This might seem to be a rather abstruse point, but it is a vital and neglected one. From it stem many of the problems that beset anyone trying to make use of the published experience of others. Research findings have not been so much contradictory as unrelated to each other, as the researchers have begun with different conceptual schemes.

Some of these have certainly been too simple in outlook. Traditional descriptions of the work of managers have been seriously defective because of a failure to appreciate this. The description that has been most widely accepted is that of a manager as a person who plans, organises and controls. The resulting picture is one of a smooth process of control. In fact, it would be very difficult to find a job which fitted this description. Not by accident, the description comes much closer to the work of a power station engineer than that of a manager.

Much more realistically, one well-known writer, Rosemary Stewart, comments: 'The picture that emerges from studies of what managers do is of someone who lives in a whirl of activity, in which attention must be switched every few minutes from one subject, problem, and person to another; of an uncertain world where relevant information includes gossip and speculation about how other people are thinking and what they are likely to do; and where it is necessary, particularly in the more senior posts, to develop a network of people who can fill one in on what is going on and what is likely to happen. It is a picture, too, not of a manager who sits quietly controlling but who is dependent upon many people, other than subordinates, with whom reciprocating relationships should be created; who needs to learn how to trade, bargain, and compromise; and a picture of managers who, increasingly as they ascend the management ladder, live in a political world where they must learn how to influence people other than subordinates, how to manoeuvre, and how to enlist support for what they want to do. In short, it is a much more human activity than that commonly suggested in management textbooks.'

The reader is invited to decide how far this description fits his experience. Overall, the point to be made is that any job description is a simplification of what actually occurs — an abstraction from the confusion of everyday life. One has to be careful not to be too abstract; not to leave out so much that the essential nature of the job is distorted. On the other hand, realism must not be allowed to override the need for simplicity. It is possible to describe any job at great length, but to be useful a description needs to be brief. Beyond a certain length the exercise becomes self-defeating as the assessors will be unable to keep it in mind.

Because of these difficulties, there is something to be said for not attempting to describe a job but simply to specify the qualities that an organisation wants in its managers. This may be possible for some, but generally there are practical difficulties in adopting this tactic. In essence these are the same as those already encountered in the storeman example. The same unrealistic kind of list of qualities soon emerges.

It is possible to talk to a normally competent manager of apparently sensible disposition and be taken aback by the list of qualities he regards as essential for the job and which, by implication, he supposes himself to possess. This, again, is not to be merely critical. A sensitive enquirer must understand the need most people have to see their work in terms which he will find romantic. The tendency is not unknown even among occupational psychologists. It must be respected, but at the same time, a realistic and simple description must be produced to be useful. From this point of view, intelligence, persuasiveness, drive, reliability and the like make sense. Foresight, generosity of outlook, empathy and the like show signs of being difficult to appraise in an assessment procedure. Charisma, vision and entrepreneurial spirit go beyond the limits of what is possible to look for in such a context.

Further, the sheer number of qualities suggested makes the problem even greater. A list of one hundred can soon be compiled. Larger ones are not uncommon. This is clearly an impossible situation.

Because of these difficulties, the most thorough selection techniques — that is those using assessment centres, use a job description compiled by professionals who take the time to observe what managers do, rather than seeking their opinions on the qualities they need to do it. Alternatively they may adopt techniques which involve managers keeping diaries of their activities or the examination of critical incidents where managers feel that their quality has been most tested. There are statistical techniques — such as factor analysis — to reduce a large number of apparent activities and consequent requirements to a usable number.

This, of course, is expensive and may be grossly cost-ineffective for the small organisation or when a single position is to be filled. Then the user has to rely on his own judgement to achieve a simple description. This is best done by means of a list of activities and the extent to which the manager will be involved in them. Possible activities are:

Managing staff
Managing labour
Negotiating (with lawyers, taxmen, customers etc.)
Giving presentations
Writing papers
Writing letters
Analysing numerical data
Placing contracts

and so on.

The activities listed are a long way short of exhaustive and they may well overlap in some cases. The essential requirement for any such list is that it should be brief, realistic and that the inevitable overlap should be kept to the practical minimum. In this way a useful job description can be derived. (Although it must be observed in passing that the notion of 'job' is now a highly abstract one, some distance from the original meaning. But it is generally used and no more convenient term is available.)

Qualities and rating scales

From a job description, assessment moves to consideration of the qualities required to do that job — a person specification. Here again two principles have to be held in mind. The first, manifestly, is realism. The second, equally important, is simplicity. Specifications for the kind of person wanted can easily become too long for assessors to hold in mind comfortably. More seriously they will be unable to find an individual to whom it applies. It is something of a joke among selectors that no one could ever live up to a description of the qualities required for any job. But this depends on the way the description is used. Looking for strength in every quality mentioned, would rule out every candidate an assessor is likely to come across. What an assessor has to look for is an acceptable balance of strengths among the qualities described.

This does, however, require that the description must be prepared with a strong degree of realism. It is necessary to think carefully about what the job involves and set out the demands accordingly. Any tendency to think in terms of the ideal must be firmly resisted.

For any job there may be, first of all, some simple physical requirements. In some, where the public need to be impressed, a minimum height may be specified. In some jobs freedom from colour-blindness — which afflicts a surprisingly high percentage of the male population — may be necessary. Good health is a near-universal requirement. A driving licence is often necessary.

After such basic requirements, an assessor needs to find out if a candidate is clever enough, can communicate adequately and has the right kind of personality. In more detail, the requirements for a trainee for senior management might read:

> The candidate must be bright enough to be able to extract the salient points from a normally complex situation, to have ideas on improved working and to be able to judge what is important and what is workable. He should be able to exercise these qualities using numerical as well as verbal information.
>
> He must communicate effectively in speech and writing.
>
> He should be reasonably likeable and able to work with others.
>
> He should be able to present a case persuasively and get others to see things his way.
>
> He needs to be energetic and enterprising and to show staying power with longer term aims.
>
> He must be capable of doing a good job, despite the stresses of work and life in general.
>
> He should be adaptable and able to grow into progressively more responsible jobs.

The problem with such specifications is that they are difficult to hold in mind while engaged in assessing. The efficient way of so concentrating the mind is by use of a rating scale. An example of one such, incorporating the qualities just described, is given on page 24. Such a device is the most graphic and convenient way of remembering the qualities that have to be looked at during assessment and it will be useful later in explaining a number of issues. This example is also a convenient method of explaining some features common to such scales. But first the simple mechanics of its use should be explained.

Figure 3.1: Rating Scale

Name................ Ref No...............

1. Penetration	7	6	5	4	3	2	1
2. Constructive Thinking	7	6	5	4	3	2	1
3. Judgement	7	6	5	4	3	2	1
4. Numeracy	7	6	5	4	3	2	1
5. Writing	7	6	5	4	3	2	1
6. Speaking	7	6	5	4	3	2	1
7. Working Relations	7	6	5	4	3	2	1
8. Influence	7	6	5	4	3	2	1
9. Drive and Determination	7	6	5	4	3	2	1
10. Reliability	7	6	5	4	3	2	1
11. Capacity for Growth	7	6	5	4	3	2	1

Final mark...................

(Signed)......................Assessor

'4' represents the average candidate, '7' an outstandingly good candidate and 1 a very poor one. The range in which candidates are to be judged is that of all candidates for the job.

(This is a rating scale for use with candidates who are to be assessed as potentially fitted for top management in due course and for this reason maximum attention is given to intellectual quality. The scale is adaptable for other appointments and, in particular, the first three qualities might be collapsed under one heading, such as 'intellectual quality'.)

The scale shows eleven qualities found to be relevant for trainees for higher management — that is, generally speaking people at the graduate level without appropriate work experience. An assessor rates a candidate for each quality by ringing one of the numbers. '4' is the rating to be given to a candidate who is average for the quality concerned. So taking 'judgement' for example, an average, sensible candidate will be rated as '4', a very silly one will get '1' and the rare person with an almost impeccable judgement will rated as '7'.

These qualities are discussed in detail in chapter 5. For the moment it is most convenient to define them in terms of their extreme values on the scale and to note any alternative terms. Some of these alternatives are narrower in scope, but may be more relevant for particular situations.

Penetration

7: Unusual ability to get to the roots of a problem.
1: Can only present a superficial view.
Alternatives: mental sharpness, quickness in the uptake.

Constructive thinking

7: Can nearly always produce a constructive new approach to a problem.
1: Hidebound in his thinking.
Alternatives: creative thinking, fertility of ideas, innovative thinking, (more narrowly) lateral thinking.

Judgement

7: Weighs evidence accurately, knows what is possible.
1. Silly, unrealistic, irrational.
Alternatives: (more narrowly) savvy, common-sense.

Numeracy

7: Easily interprets and explains numerical information.
1: Baffled by numerical information.

Writing

7: Well-organised, precise, clear, easy to read.
1: Poorly put together, obscure, turgid.

Speaking

7: Fluent, clear, precise, interesting.
1: Stumbling, obscure, sloppy, lifeless.
Alternatives: (more narrowly) word-power, fluency.

Working Relations

7: Sensitive to others, liked, respected, very easy to work with.
1: Insensitive, unpopular, ignored, impossible to work with.
Alternatives: likeability, personal contacts (more narrowly) interpersonal skills

Influence

7: Easily sells ideas to others.
1: No influence, counterproductive.
Alternatives: (more narrowly) customer relations, ability to sell ideas, persuasiveness.

Drive and Determination

7: Energetic, enterprising, great staying power.
1: Lazy, complacent, gives up easily.
Alternatives: energy, enterprise, staying-power (more narrowly) motivation

Reliability

7: Nearly always gets the job done no matter what the difficulties.
1: Gives way at any difficulty.
Alternatives: (more narrowly) resistance to stress, resilience (historically) emotional stability.

Capacity for Growth

7: Eager for new responsibilities, receptive to counsel.
1: Resists change, defensive reaction to counsel.
Alternatives: potential, adaptability (more narrowly) self-knowledge.

As already stated, these are the extreme cases and therefore by definition candidates meriting such ratings on every quality will hardly ever be encountered. But these reference points at the end of the scale make it easier to use the others; rating candidates as above or below average, or well-above or below average.

The scale shown is one suitable for the selection of management trainees who are expected to move eventually to the top jobs in the organisation and who are selected by means of an assessment centre. Because these use job simulations, which in general terms are the best predictors of long-term managerial performance, the scale analyses intellectual performance in detail. This is not only because such factors are important for long term development, but because the job simulations give a great deal of evidence in this area and to use this evidence efficiently such detail is necessary. With a less intellectually demanding job these could be reduced to one item such as 'intellectual ability'; with a less thorough procedure such a condensation may be a practical necessity.

The scale is also useful in illustrating the general point that assessors can seldom find outstanding strength in all qualities and, for each individual candidate, it shows the balance of strengths in a practical way.

This example is also about the right length for effective assessment. Any such form is bound to be arbitrary to some degree. It is easy to think of qualities that might be added, but such a scale soon becomes unwieldy. Experience in a number of different organisations suggests that round about a dozen qualities are enough to give fair coverage and yet not become too long for the mind to grasp. With more, decision makers tend to concentrate on a subset of such factors with a consequent loss of efficiency, particularly when they are not aware of the way in which they are

Figure 3.2: Specimen rating scales for use in simpler procedures

Research Scientist

1. Good professional knowledge and skill	1	2	3	4	5	Knowledge poor, lacks skill
2. Intelligent	1	2	3	4	5	Not intelligent
3. Reflective, can think a problem through	1	2	3	4	5	Can't think through a problem
4. Creative — has original ideas	1	2	3	4	5	No original ideas
5. Numerate	1	2	3	4	5	Non-numerate
6. Perseveres, does not give up easily	1	2	3	4	5	Easily gives up
7. Methodical, well organised	1	2	3	4	5	Slapdash, ill-organised

Check list of other qualities to be considered when appropriate

potential	organising ability
adaptability	social skills
maturity	decisiveness
understanding of others	breadth of outlook
health	acceptance of responsibility
suitability for management development	

Salesman

1. Talks well, fluent and assured	1	2	3	4	5	Speech stumbling, lacks conviction
2. Persuasive, gets his way	1	2	3	4	5	No powers of persuasion
3. Practical, sees where the chances lie	1	2	3	4	5	Remote, impractical
4. Keen on money	1	2	3	4	5	Money no incentive
5. Energetic, gets around	1	2	3	4	5	Lazy, unadventurous
6. Perseveres, does not give up easily	1	2	3	4	5	Easily gives up
7. Resilient, self-confident	1	2	3	4	5	Easily upset, lacks confidence

simplifying the problem. Cattell, a psychologist, was able to reduce all the 60,000 terms used to describe personality to 16, so that simplification of any list is clearly possible. Some organisations use fewer qualities. AT&T, which has pioneered selection methods in the USA, begins with 26 headings reduced to 8 by statistical analysis. Sears Roebuck begins with 40 which reduce to 9.

Other more appropriate scales need to be used for scientific, professional and technical appointments and the length and refinement of the rating scale will vary with the length of the selection process. The suggested scale is appropriate for an assessment centre procedure lasting more than a day. It would be unwise to expect to cover the items thoroughly in a half-hour interview, and a simpler scale would be more useful.

Such scales are a convenience, and like all such must be used with understanding.

1. They ensure that the major areas have been covered.
2. They allow easy comparisons between different candidates.

But

3. They are not exhaustive. In individual cases, qualities not mentioned on the scale may be of great, even decisive, importance. These are not to be ignored because they are not represented.

A useful device, particularly with a short procedure which has to be limited to obvious essentials, is a check list of other qualities that might emerge or turn out to be significant for a particular candidate (see example on page 27).

Generally speaking, a 5 or 7 point scale is to be preferred. These both provide for an 'average' rating. Five points are probably better for a simple assessment, but 7 are to be preferred for a rigorous one. People can be reluctant to use extreme values, and a 7 point scale ensures that assessments are at least spread over 5 points.

A further issue to bear in mind is that specifications should not either be too general or too specific and detailed. 'Management ability', for example, is too general. This is the quality that a specification attempts to analyse. Qualities such as 'dependence on others' or 'dominance' are generally too detailed to fit into a balanced scheme. Even more importantly, they overlook the fact that different people do a job in different ways with equal degrees of success. One individual may manage his staff largely by setting a clear example. Another may work equally effectively by taking time to tell them what is required. One salesman may pressure customers into buying. Another will prefer a more persuasive approach. Any specification should allow for such different approaches.

Some possible headings have been omitted. Some which would be appropriate for other types of job include 'professional (or technical) knowledge', 'professional skill', 'experience', 'appearance and bearing'. Some have been omitted because the writer does not understand them, although they have been used by some organisations: 'helicopter ability' and 'overall executive orientation'.

Others are more appropriate for the assessment of people with some experience, especially where reports on this are available to the assessors: 'profit orientation', 'organising ability', 'understanding of company ethos' are among them. With such people 'maturity' would be increasingly more appropriate than 'capacity for growth'.

Some are best avoided; either because they are romantic rather than realistic or imprecise or both. 'dynamic', 'abrasive' and 'aggressive' are prime examples. The last term has considerable sales appeal but the dictionary more prosaically defines 'aggressive' as 'quarrelsome, belligerent, assertive, vigorous'. Manifestly, there can be few jobs for the quarrelsome or belligerent in an efficiently run organisation. If, on the other hand, vigour is the quality required, it would be better to use the term explicitly. 'Abrasive' has been widely used, but manifestly a person with this characteristic will not be a welcome member of an organisation. In a moribund one which is to be revived, such a person may have his place, but then the term prescribes the approach to be adopted to revivification when others may be more efficient.

A more complex case is that of 'leadership'. There is no doubt that this may refer to some highly desirable qualities, but at the same time it can lead to dangerous misunderstandings. Firstly, the term is naturally interpreted by many in terms of the dashing infantry subaltern, who could be quite the wrong person for many organisations. But, more insidiously, the person who becomes the leader in a group discussion at selection is simply the person who is most gifted in discussion and by no means the person who will exercise leadership in more relevant situations.

This is a particular case of an important research finding, namely that the person who becomes the leader of a group is the one who is best able to help it achieve its needs. If the group faces a financial problem, an accountant is most likely to take control. If the problem is legal, a lawyer will be in the best position to do so. It takes a situation of physical danger, of the sort that most organisations will not come across, for the soldier to be best suited to lead the group.

For these reasons, and particularly the last, the functions covered by this term are best identified in a way that relates to the needs of the organisation concerned. If the need is to manage a labour force or train a group of bright novice accountants or to co-ordinate the activities of a group of social workers it is best described in those terms.

(It has been argued that since any organisation must contain few leaders and many followers, most people should be tested for 'followership'. Harvard Business School once offered a course designed to teach this activity. Only a few percent of those eligible entered; 'leadership' attracted nearly 100 per cent.)

A common and related assumption is that a manager is an entrepreneur, with the entrepreneur then seen as someone with the qualities of a market trader. Thus the vital qualities become push, competitiveness and cheek. Such a picture carries with it a dedication to pursuing personal interests with a patent disregard for those of others. There are jobs like these — on the trading floor of a currency exchange, for example — but almost by definition an organisation cannot survive if it contains any significant number of people with these qualities. Barristers in chambers probably represent the nearest approach to such an organisation. There, a number of individuals in a highly competitive market co-operate to provide themselves with basic services — a very limited form of organisation. Sales organisations regulate competition by giving their salesmen different territories, but then the salesmen are better seen as individuals employed by the organisation, rather than as people for making the organisation work.

None of this is to say that an organisation cannot accommodate a few such egocentric people, and if such a person is seen as having particular qualities that are rare or of outstanding usefulness, he can be appointed with open eyes about his drawbacks. More generally, successful managers may have something of the entrepreneur in them, but this will seldom be their prime activity.

Assessment redefined

This brief excursion into the design of rating scales makes it possible to redefine the job of assessment in practical terms. In essence, we are examining the evidence to find reasons for rating the candidate as 'above average' or 'below average'. Before we have any information about the candidate, the simplest and most accurate assumption we can make is that he is average in all respects. As we acquire evidence we can structure and use it by making provisional assessments of below or above average on the scale. And we can adjust them as more and more evidence is collected. This should not be taken to imply that an assessor should strain to move the candidate's rating from the average point. He should not. Many people are average for many qualities. Many more are average for some. And if the assessor is in genuine doubt, he is doing the least damage to his overall estimate if he stays on the average rating for a particular quality.

At the same time he must interpret the terms on the rating scale in relation to the job to be done. Judgement, for example, is a different sort of quality for administrators and engineers, and an assessor would not discuss the same topics with a chemist and an actuary in order to decide their degree of penetration. These two devices — rating scale and job description — must be employed in harmony, using one to make sense of the other.

Traits

Rating scales such as those shown here make a vital point in an implicit way. This is that people are fairly complex, and when we describe them in terms of traits as 'honest', 'clever','reliable' and the like we must not form too simple ideas of what we are saying. When we are children we tend to think that, when someone is said to be clever, this means that they are clever in every conceivable situation. As we grow up we learn that this is not so. Someone can be very clever academically but hopeless at managing financial affairs or totally unable to understand how a car works. Conversely, many people who can understand complex systems for betting on horses or filling in football pools have done very badly at school. An assessor cannot, therefore, conclude that because people are found to be sensible, reliable or energetic in one particular situation, they will be so in all situations.

What we do is to strike some sort of average across a range of situations and then use this average to predict the way the candidate will behave in novel situations. If, for example, someone has been energetic in sport, travel, vacation jobs and academic work, then it is a fair inference that he will be an energetic member of the organisation. This, of course, is not necessarily so. There have been cases of people who were energetic at first, but slackened off once they achieved security. In one case, an energetic man apparently found it impossible to sit at a desk and work. But to suggest that such cases discredit the approach is simply to demand infallibility. And, as the reader knows, there is no such thing in human affairs. Once an assessor has weighed all the evidence he has done all that can be done to make such a judgement.

A rating scale makes the logic of such assessments clear. It implicitly makes the point that people are not, for example, totally reliable or totally unreliable, but reliable in varying degrees. It therefore discourages any tendency to think otherwise. It also by-passes the psychological theories which have grown from this tendency to insist that, despite all appearances to the contrary, people do behave consistently in every kind of situation.

The halo effect

It has been demonstrated that judgement of these qualities is not as independent as it should be. It has been shown, for example, that interviewers overrate the intelligence of people they like. Most people overrate the intelligence of people wearing glasses at the first meeting. That is, observing that people possess one quality or feature, they assume that they have some other unobserved one. This is clearly undesirable. In these particular instances an independent check is possible. But for many of the qualities to be assessed — drive, reliability and the like — there is no independent check. Statistical analysis has suggested that many correlations between judgements of these qualities are suspiciously high, suggesting that they have not been made independently but have influenced each other. (However, such statistical measures alone can never establish that such an error has occurred.) Consultations between assessors may show discrepancies of judgement between them, which may lead to re-examination of initial ratings but this may still leave the question of who is the more accurate.

The way of avoiding this kind of mistake is again by

self-awareness on the part of the assessors. If we know that we are liable to overrate the judgement of those we like or the drive of those who show a lively response in an interview, we can guard against such mistakes. We can also be aware that we tend to like those whose judgement we rate favourably, but this is reasonable enough. In the discussions which follow, some likely halo effects are identified. The assessor, aware of these tendencies, is equipped to observe and correct them.

Summary

This chapter has dealt with the devices essential for efficient selection — a description of a job and a specification for a person who could do it. These must be simple and realistic so that assessors are able to keep them in mind and to allow for human individuality — the fact that different people will do the same job in different ways. This last requirement also means that the descriptions must be at the right level of generality — analytic to some degree, but not so detailed as to prescribe the way in which the job is to be done. For those without previous experience of work it is important to assess basic traits and not features of behaviour which can be learned after appointment.

While working at assessment the person specification is most conveniently represented by a rating scale. Some useful forms have been presented and discussed.

The danger of confusing one quality with another — the 'halo effect' — has been described.

4

Methods — the Sources of Evidence

The possible sources of evidence are:

1. Application form.
2. References.
3. Internal reports — a routine staff report or one designed especially for the assessment.
4. Tests such as those of intelligence, numeracy, vocabulary and the like.
5. Practical tests which simulate some of the jobs to be done in the organisation — tactful letters, in-tray exercises and group exercises.
6. Personality tests.
7. Interviews.

These sources are combined or sometimes used alone to provide methods of selection. Since the prime method is interviewing and this is a complex subject, it is placed in a chapter of its own. The first chapter is concerned with sources and methods based on paper and the third chapter looks at two alternative responses to the problems associated with interviewing.

The amount of evidence an assessor will have in any particular situation will vary. As far as the number of sources is concerned he will probably have most at the recruitment stage. For job assignments the quality of the evidence from staff reports and work record should be significantly higher.

4.1 Paper-based

Self-selection

This is not usually regarded as a selection method, but it is probably the most important and cost-effective of all. A great deal of trouble is saved if the people who apply have selected themselves as likely runners and a great deal may be lost if promising people do not see the job as one for which they might be suitable.

A realistic description of the job and the organisation is therefore particularly important because it enables the candidate to make his own judgement on whether he is suitable for it. Far too often candidates turn up for a job interview, knowing little about the job and uncertain whether they really want it. They may learn things about the organisation or the job itself during the interview which make them decide that they do not want it. This is clearly expensive for all concerned and repeated too often may do the organisation's reputation no good.

An advertisement which does not describe the job precisely may either fail to attract candidates or bring in a large number who are then found to be unsuitable. There is a natural and understandable tendency to sell the job to potential applicants in language of consumer advertising.

> Wanted qualified and dynamic accountant with powers of leadership to head-up a highly motivated team in progressive company. A highly competitive salary will be paid to the right applicant.

This typical enough example says nothing. It may appeal to those with delusions of career grandeur, but it will do nothing to help individuals decide if they are what the organisation is really looking for. Phrases like 'will manage the work of four clerks' may lack glamour, but will tell potential applicants what is required of them.

Some features of a job may be attractive to some applicants but not to others. For example, many people can find a job with a lot of travel stimulating. Others simply do not want to spend time away from home, so that if travel is part of the job the requirements should be set out clearly.

Features which many would find unattractive can be mentioned with tact. 'This position will involve frequent negotiations with tax officials' will warn off those who dislike confrontations. 'A rapidly expanding company' will describe a situation attractive to those looking for early advancement and warn off anyone looking for a settled environment.

So the advertised description can make a useful contribution to the cost-effectiveness of the selection process, by helping the candidate to select himself. Advertising has its limitations, however, and some organisations invite the candidate to an informal interview where he can learn about the organisation and his potential place in it.

Application forms

These generally speaking are under-rated selection instruments. Far too often they appear to be designed — if that is the word — by a junior clerk or secretary. Some organisations send out forms that are successful as artistic productions, but are otherwise inadequate. On one form the writer came across, the candidate had room to write his name five times over but had so little space to write in his academic qualifications that the result was often illegible.

Such forms are necessary to avoid having to work from letters of application. These not only omit useful information but appear in a variety of styles ranging from the barely legible written on scraps of paper to many type-written pages of inflated self-selling.

Some thought is necessary as to what is wanted from such a form. Firstly, there are the necessary details such as surname, forenames, date of birth and the like. Normal address and any temporary address for correspondence should be allowed for, with phone numbers and styles of address (Mr, Mrs, Miss, Ms, Dr).

After that much depends on the job, but normally academic qualifications are necessary. These will include schools and universities attended, with results obtained. For most management jobs school leaving results (American 'Advanced Placement Examination', 'SATs' and 'ACTs'; Scottish 'Highers' and 'A' levels in the rest of the UK), degree results and higher degrees will be sufficient. But when someone with an arts degree is being considered for an accountancy job or the like, it is useful to check that they have a basic knowledge of mathematics. An organisation that sends people abroad will want to know of any elementary instruction in languages if the candidate has no advanced qualifications.

The right sort of space for previous jobs should be left with a clear indication of how much detail is required. Some organisations want to know about travel and spare-time activities. A professional psychologist assessing the more difficult aspects of personality — reliability, drive and capacity for growth — will want to know the details of family background but, given the understandable sensitivity on such questions, it is probably better to give an additional form to short-listed candidates on arrival at the selection procedure.

Space should be provided for details of any previous applications to the organisation, the post involved and the stage reached. Times at which the candidate cannot attend the selection process should be asked for.

Form design is a minor technology in its own right and most large organisations will have an expert on the subject who will always be worth consulting. For a smaller organisation this is clearly impossible and the sensible thing is to try a draft of the proposed form on a few people who could be candidates. Instructions which seemed clear to the designer can be misinterpreted and replies can be longer or shorter than allowed for. Adjustment at this stage is cheap and easy and can save a great deal of later frustration. Unless it is impossible to do otherwise, instructions for completing the form should be on the form itself. Separate sheets or booklets are often carelessly read.

(The simplest approach in the UK is to get candidates to use the 'Standard Application Form' used by university careers advisory services, where it is possible to do so. This covers nearly all the points mentioned and saves the candidates' time and so that it is likely to be filled in more carefully.)

Some organisations are said to use a deliberately long and difficult application form to cut down the number of candidates and test the motivation of those who do complete it. This tactic cannot be recommended. A well designed form should provide a sound basis for deciding who is worth seeing and who is not. Form filling as a test of motivation is certainly unreliable and such a form may convey an unfavourable impression.

With the same aim some ask the candidate to state why he wants the job. The replies to such questions are of little value. Sometimes the candidate in consultation with his friends may hit on an appealing answer, but generally a direct approach to the question is not helpful (see page 94). On the other hand space for the candidate to add any experience or qualifications not otherwise covered can sometimes provide additional useful information.

Rarely will a form be used as the basis for a job offer. An experienced assessor can often make a surprisingly accurate prediction of how a candidate will fare in a selection process. But even the best quite often make disastrous predictions as well, so that even if a candidate on the other side of the world appears uniquely qualified for a specialised post, the organisation will want to make further enquiries. But a well-designed form will allow the organisation to draw up a short-list of candidates to be seen. This can be done in a common-sense way or by means of a carefully designed biodata approach.

At the selection stage application forms should be studied in detail so that assessors do not waste time during an interview asking for information which is already available. The form should be studied in detail, not only for what it says, but looking for any omissions. A candidate's failure to account for a year may simply be a clerical error. On the other hand, he might be deliberately concealing something to his discredit. Assessors must be alert to such tactics.

Biodata

A more advanced use is sometimes made of application forms. This is nowadays generally referred to as the biodata method, but in the past has been called 'The Esso method' after the firm that made extensive use of it and in the Second World War it was used as 'the weighted application blank'. There are differences in detail between these. Biodata forms usually present the candidate with a series of multiple choice questions, each answer carrying an appropriate score. With a weighted application blank, scores are given to replies on a normal application form. But whatever the details of the method, the basic logic is the same. In essence, it involves examining the histories of successful candidates before recruitment and identifying features of these which distinguish them from the unsuccessful. Among the factors that predict such success are such as having been a school prefect or captain of a sports team. Jobs such as a paper round have a predictive power.

The candidate fills in a highly detailed questionnaire which includes such achievements, spare time activities and academic qualifications. Each response is given a score, the value of which has been worked out by statistical analysis, and these scores are totalled to give an order of merit.

The method has obvious strengths, particularly in that it represents no more than a formalisation of the normal preparation of a short-list. As such it has advantages. It is more fair than less organised scrutiny, in that it is totally systematic, and the job can be done by clerks and computers rather than by expensive professional staff.

However, the first statistical analysis is expensive and the method can only be used where a fairly large intake is available for the initial analysis. Further, it is not clear that it is superior to an overall human judgement of a candidate's suitability. (The evidence on this point is ambiguous.) It certainly can be unfair to an unusual case. A more obvious limitation is that an intelligent candidate can often work out what the favourable answer is and stretch the truth — if not simply lie — to provide it. Finally it appears to impose a particularly rigid form of predestination upon candidates — to involve the assumption that those not successful at the age of 21 never will be.

A useful comment on this approach was provided by Damon Runyon, author of *Guys and Dolls*. He quotes the Biblical text: 'The race is not always to the swift or the battle to the strong. But', he adds, 'that's the way the betting goes.' The method offers a systematic way of laying the odds but apart from being unfair to some individual candidates, it may overlook some unusually promising ones. Efficient assessment needs to look beyond achievements in a short life span, at the more fundamental qualities that make for achievement in the longer run.

On the whole then, the method has its uses for reducing a large number of candidates to a manageable short-list, but few would defend it as a complete method in itself.

Preliminary tests

The reports from these should again be studied in detail. Assessors should decide what they can take for granted and what they should investigate further.

References

Candidates are usually asked to name at least one referee. Reading the resulting reports is an art in itself. One must first, however, observe that some references are too inadequate to be usable. Some colleges or schools evidently feel under no obligation to supply information about the candidates in any useful form. One can get a report which merely states that the candidate attended the institution between certain dates but that nothing can be remembered about him. This is unfortunate, but there is nothing to be done about it.

More generally, an assessor will have accounts of varying insight, complexity and frankness. Referees, as most of us know from experience, work in two frames of mind. Firstly, most are eager to give a truthful account. Secondly, most are eager to do the best for their candidate and so will emphasise strengths and put weaknesses in a less direct way. An assessor has, therefore, to interpret what he reads with some care. Thus he can read that 'Miss X is fundamentally stable' and deduce that he can expect some surface fireworks. Or he can read 'Mr Y's dedication has not always made him immediately popular with more easygoing colleagues' and be prepared to find someone who is either abrasive, egocentric or both.

Generally, referees represent the candidate in a rather favourable light and assessors have to be prepared to make some correction. On the whole, one gives most initial weight to a reference that gives a balanced account mentioning weaknesses as well as strengths. But an assessor has to be alert not only to what is said but what is missed out. A reference that does not say that a candidate is well-liked is rather unusual. There is something to be looked at in this case, though it might well be that this was simply an omission and not an evasion.

It also has to be borne in mind that many referees can be poorly informed about an organisation and its requirements. The report which ran 'I am sure that Mr Z will make an excellent member of the Diplomatic Service, but I am afraid he lacks the panache to make a good librarian' may be part of legend, but it does highlight the sort of egocentric comment that one can come across. Some references indeed tell more about the writer than the candidate. 'Despite his long hair, Mr B is a decent young man' tells one something about the writer's views on hair-styles but little about the candidate.

Just occasionally a very negative reference makes a candidate appear totally unsuitable. Very rarely one is received that appears to be written with venom. These cannot be taken at their face value any more than any other. A discreet questioning of the candidate about his relations with his referee may give an assessor the confidence to trust his own judgement.

Reading references then is an art which requires an assessor to deploy his judgement to the full. He may have to decode some rather careful statements, and be alert for omissions at vital points. If he knows the writer, or has become accustomed to his reports, then he can do this the more easily. Overall, references should be treated as a starting point for investigation. Any significant comment should be treated as a hypothesis to be investigated. No such comment should be taken for granted; none ignored.

Internal reports

For a candidate already working in the organisation there will be either a special report, a copy of his latest staff report or a report based on a series of staff reports. These need the same kind of interpretation as references do. A report writer will feel the same conflicts as a referee and resolve them in his own individual way. He may have a limited idea or an exaggerated estimate of the requirements of the new job, so that his comments may be inappropriate. In a large organisation, the personnel department will attempt to compensate for any perceived lack of balance, but often without knowledge of the individual reported on.

A further difficulty is with gradings. These cannot be taken at their face value. Commonly the majority of people are given above average gradings, so that the term loses its meaning. 'Average' in fact means 'rather bad'. And some organisations are very unhelpful to themselves in this respect. When they grade a candidate below 'excellent', they may well be pointing to a serious deficiency.

Once an assessor has read a few such reports he soon learns to give such details the proper weight. Again he can do this more precisely if he knows the report writer, or perhaps the department concerned. Generally he should note the points on which the candidate gets the highest rating and those on which he gets the lowest. He should be looking at the differential between the ratings rather than their absolute values. What he cannot do with any confidence is to compare any two candidates by means of these ratings. He has no means of equating one report writer's 'very good' with another's. This is even more likely to be the case when the candidates are from different departments. Certainly in this case, fine differences of one grade are meaningless and only gross differences can be given any weight.

The most difficult situation assessors can face is where a reporting writer has given a poor report on a candidate and this turns out to be at odds with his performance in assessment. This is a rare occurrence but when it does happen then the assessors' skill and judgement will be tested to the full. Generally, a large organisation must work on the assumption that its members will report fairly and accurately. An assessor must expect a few exceptions to this, but he must be extremely cautious before deciding that he has come across one. Much may depend on the point of difference in assessment.

Testing procedures give an estimate of a candidate's intellectual powers in which an assessor can have a high degree of confidence. If these are treated dismissively in a report, he can rely on his own assessment especially if he then judges that the candidate has been intellectually underemployed. At the other end of the scale, where a candidate is reported as being low on determination or reliability, the situation is much more difficult. Any evidence the assessors can uncover will be indirect, and they would need strong evidence to override such a report.

Speculation about a report writer's motives gets nowhere. An assessor can always think up a likely explanation but he has no means of verifying it. He should question the candidate discreetly about his relationship with his reporting officer and if this is antagonistic, he would have more justification for putting weight on his own conclusions. In this situation, as in assessment generally, there are no simple rules which an assessor can follow with safety. He has to use all his judgement and all his caution in interpreting the evidence.

Tests

Tests of intelligence are discussed in a later chapter where it is more convenient to do so.

Practical tests

These may take different forms but are designed to represent tasks which will actually be performed in a job. The simplest are typing tests and the like. These call for little or no interpretation. At the other end of the scale, there are the complex simulation tests, such as the in-basket and group tests used in assessment centres, where a great deal depends on the judgement of the assessor.

Rules for exercising such judgement cannot be laid down. The assessor will need all the skill and experience developed in his working life in order to arrive at his verdict. It is important to realise that candidates come to such tests with vastly different degrees of experience and training. Some will come to a written exercise having been carefully coached in the art of essay writing. Others may not have written an essay for several years. An assessor must mark the written work in accordance with the performance he sees. But he should also note any clear evidence of lack of relevant training. This could be an important piece of evidence for the final assessment. Similarly, with a committee simulation there will be some candidates with experience of such work and others who have never sat on a committee. The assessor would do well to note such differences.

Personality tests

These are pencil and paper tests, where candidates answer questions about themselves.

These tests, the designers claim, will assess aspects of a candidate's personality or, in some cases, give a complete account of it. There are also various kinds of inventories in which candidates are asked to list the significant facts of their personal histories or their interests.

As sources of information these are subject to the same limitations as candidates' interview accounts of themselves. This is not to deny that they have their uses. For people who wish to understand themselves better in order to receive vocational guidance or psychotherapeutic help they have an established use, but these are situations where the tester and the tested are co-operating in the latter's attempts at self-understanding. In selection and similar activities, the situation is rather different. It is a bargaining rather than a co-operative one. The tester is in effect saying that he will give a prize (a job) for the right answers. The candidate will therefore be likely to attempt to supply these rather than reply sincerely. There are those who claim that the candidate cannot work out what the winning answers are, but these claims cannot be given much weight. And, in addition, intelligent young people find it difficult to take some of the questions seriously and may answer facetiously.

Because of the obvious economy of such pencil and paper tests, many find it convenient to ignore these facts and treat the answers they get as useful precise data. This means that the onus is then on them to show that the test results are valid — that the tests assess those aspects of personality which they claim to. This has not been done.

As a preliminary to an interview, many organisations ask candidates to describe themselves, their experiences, achievements, work and what they have found difficult and so on. They may ask for such descriptions as essays or provide forms of varying complexity. The usefulness of such questions is something assessors can decide in the light of their experience of using them.

Summary

This section has described the paper methods that are available and has argued that they should be regarded as short-listing devices and as aids to a full selection procedure.

4.2 The interview

Nearly every selection procedure includes an interview. Impressions made there often carry major, if not decisive, weight. This is understandable as interviews have many advantages. Perhaps the most obvious — so obvious that it is seldom mentioned in the text-books — is that meeting a candidate helps one organise and make sense of all that one has read about him. The most careful study of application forms, references and the like leaves a rather faint general impression of the candidate. Seeing him sharpens the impression; the word is usefully made flesh. Assessors can think about his qualities in a much more concrete way. They are, conversely, a useful way of giving a more concrete idea of the job to the candidate.

Preliminary interviews

These can take place before a formal application is made or after a short list has been drawn up from such applications. Apart from a description of the job, which is best given by someone on his likely working level, a candidate should have every opportunity to ask all the questions he wants. This might seem expensive, but in the longer run, it can greatly add to the efficiency of selection by ensuring that those who decide to apply have a clear idea of what they are applying for.

Obviously economics favours restricting such interviews to short-listed candidates. But when students, in particular, are being recruited for a general entry scheme, it may be necessary to spend more. The reader, on learning that the average student spends something like twenty minutes reading printed information about an organisation before deciding whether to apply to it, might shrug his shoulders at the irresponsibility of youth or the state of university education, but those engaged in recruitment at this level have to take this as their starting point. Students are not taught what to look for in a job and often do not know what questions they ought to ask. And there is a limit to what people are willing to accept from written descriptions. 'Milk round' interviews, visiting students on their home ground, can be well worthwhile. A visit from a member of an organisation with an opportunity for informal discussion of the job can be very useful to both parties. And, of course, such interviews are frequently used to short-list candidates.

The selection interview

Selection interviews have further important advantages. Major among these is the fact that interviewing is a two-way process. Here, unlike other testing situations — written examinations and the like — the candidate can always say that he does not understand a question or say that he thinks it is inappropriate. He can qualify a first answer or suggest that the interviewer has placed a false construction on it. For this sort of reason an interview is of great value.

Further, it provides a means of finding out about a candidate's personality — normally something that would not otherwise be possible.

However, in practice, interviews have an enormous drawback. As they are normally conducted by untrained assessors they give very inaccurate results. This has been established in many surveys and reports on how interviewing is carried out. It is difficult to report some of these without appearing to have abandoned sober comment and to have descended into farce.

In one UK city candidates for the post of Chief Constable were required to appear in morning dress before the entire council and answer four questions which they found printed on a card in front of them on the rostrum. A prospective teacher had to appear in front of a huge committee of thirty, each of whom asked her a question of their own choice in turn. In another case, an interviewer announced that he had to make an urgent phone-call and then could be overheard doing so on a trivial matter. Assessors who neglect to have the candidates' papers ready in front of them are too common to merit any surprise.

The experienced assessor who is asked to advise a candidate on how to make the most of himself is in a difficult position. It is not difficult to tell him what a good interviewer will be looking for, but the odds are that the candidate will meet someone who does not know how to do the job. Common comments have been 'He didn't seem to know what to ask' and 'He told me about himself most of the time.' It is not unreasonable to advise a person in this situation to have a go as he might well get the job by mistake, if not on his merits — especially if he can put on a good selling performance.

Sadly, this means that the candidate who wishes to succeed would do well to study the procedures of some tribal societies, where young men have to appear in front of the elders and demonstrate that they understand the rules of adult life in the tribe and their place in it. His safest bet is that his assessors are seeking a similar kind of reassurance and seek to demonstrate that he will fit in with their organisation. A candidate who can produce confident answers to the questions thrown at him while exhibiting the proper degree of deference to his questioners will go far. (His questioners being the final judges of what constitutes the proper degree). One who hesitates, flounders, is too assertive or obsequious stands a poor chance. There is a ritual to be gone through and a candidate who can play his part in it is the one most likely to succeed.

This might be thought an exaggerated account, but it has been surpassed. It has been seriously suggested that selection is largely a matter of establishing that a candidate will fit into the culture of an organisation. The recommended method would culminate in a session where the candidate and his assessors reach a mutual decision on his suitability.

But more to our present point are the several hundred studies which have shown how even interviews conducted by sensible people, with a thorough knowledge of the job applied for, have gone wrong.

These it should be emphasised, are interviews given by experienced managers, salesmen and academics — people experienced in their business and experienced in dealing with people. All could reasonably claim that they interviewed on every day of their working lives. However, interviewing for assessment is a different sort of activity from those of persuading, selling, disciplining, inspiring or reassuring. Indeed some of the habits acquired in developing these skills can be a definite handicap during assessment.

It is instructive to watch a group of untrained interviewers at work. Ignoring the person who conducts a close check on the application form - 'Your name is John Jones?', 'Your age is 23?', 'You live in Rugby?' and so on — an observer usually sees a series of questions of varying degrees of relevance, which may tell him more about the questioner than the replies do about the candidate.

Afterwards, there will be a discussion in which confident judgements will be delivered on the candidate's energy, trustworthiness, ability to cope with stress and the like. Quite often they are based on a minute examination of the verbal form of the candidates replies ('He hesitated when you asked him if he liked hard work') rather than any more solid evidence. They might explain that they are 'putting the candidate through his paces' and seeing how he 'shapes up'. This mystical explanation is inadequate and so is the procedure it purports to describe.

The purpose of an interview is to obtain evidence. This might seem to be the emptiest of cliches. But anyone who has watched such a group of able people engage a candidate in amiable conversation for half an hour and then deliver themselves of confident opinions on the candidate's personality will not see it in this dismissive light. And if this experience has been many times repeated, he will know that he is making an important point.

A lack of purpose accounts for a large part of the failure of interviews. The job is to see if the candidate is clever enough, can communicate and whether he has a personality suitable for the job. This cannot possibly be established by random questioning. Careful planning and skilled questioning are necessary. And to achieve the best results the assessors must strike up the right sort of relationship with the interviewee. So the manner, technique and content of the interview must all be right. For ease of exposition these will be treated in turn, but such a separation is for convenience only. In the interview itself these are interdependent aspects of the same process.

Manner

An interview must not be an interrogation. To get the best response from the candidate, it is necessary to develop a sympathetic and understanding relationship with the candidate — to develop rapport. Unless he is put at relative ease, he is unlikely to reveal much of value. The ease is relative because the candidate must be ready to think hard and quickly at times. But he should be able to feel that he is doing so in an atmosphere where he will be able to demonstrate his worth and where any weaker points will be seen in their proper place, in the overall context of his qualities, and not exploited to his discomfort.

This alone makes the interviewer's job difficult. While conducting an apparently friendly conversation, he has to extract evidence with all the sense of purpose that he would bring to a straightforward interrogation. Many interviews fail because the right atmosphere is not developed; as many fail because the interviewer does not want to spoil the atmosphere by asking awkward questions. But awkward questions must be asked and they can be, while maintaining a sympathetic approach. Getting the balance right, however, calls for a lot of skill and this can only be developed with experience.

As always in developing a relationship there are rules which should be followed and there are occasions when the rules may have to be broken. Generally, for example, the interviewer will begin with a few genial preliminaries and an easy question. Most candidates will respond favourably to such an approach. A highly nervous one, however, may grow more nervous as a result of such obvious preliminaries. In such a case, a brisk approach to the matter in hand will run the lesser risk.

A more dramatic but less frequent example of how rules need to be broken is provided by smiling. Generally a smile will help put the candidate at ease and supply encouragement, but sometimes it will have the opposite effect. This can be very disconcerting for the interviewer, who may be baffled by the reaction he gets. The reason for a negative response is interesting. It was revealed by a series of experiments in which subjects were shown photographs of various facial expressions such as rage, disdain, friendliness and so on. It was found that people had difficulty in distinguishing a friendly smiling expression from one showing contempt; some naturally suspicious people found the distinction impossible.

So if the interviewer knows that the candidate is that sort of person or that he is suspicious of the proceedings, he should break the rule and present a solemn face. If a smile brings a disconcerting response, this again is the likely explanation and again gravity is the best policy.

Recognising situations such as this can strain the skill and resourcefulness of highly experienced assessors and newcomers should not be unduly cast down by the occasional failure to develop rapport. An interviewer sometimes has to accept such a situation after having made every effort to gain a candidate's confidence.

The need for tact in questioning needs no emphasis but it should be appreciated that it has two aspects — wording and timing. Few would think of starting an interview with a question such as 'Why was your degree so bad?'. The right way to get a useful answer is to wait until a good rapport has been developed and then ask the question in a neutral way — such as 'How did you feel about your degree result?' This will enable the candidate to be self-critical without a loss of face.

Tact is not a reason for avoiding awkward questions and must not be used as an excuse for avoiding any question that is relevant. A candidate may be painfully aware of some fact to his apparent discredit and will expect to be asked about it. It is often a relief to be able to do so in a sympathetic atmosphere. In one case a girl had a poor exam result, but was able to tell the interviewer that her mother had been dying of cancer and that she had helped with the nursing. The assessors decided that the episode was to her credit as a human being and that the exam result should not be taken as a final guide to her intellectual abilities. A period of long unemployment may look suspicious, but there may be good reasons for it — illness or accident among them. One candidate was evasive when talking about his family background to the point where his assessors became worried about his honesty. But sympathetic questioning led to the admission that he was illegitimate and was afraid that this would be held against him. Assured that this was totally unimportant he was greatly relieved and co-operated fully for the rest of the interview in a pleasant and open way. Cases such as this are not uncommon.

No relevant questions should therefore be shirked because they are difficult, but there are two invariable rules for putting them. Firstly, if the candidate challenges the interviewer's right to ask any question, the interviewer must be ready to explain clearly and convincingly why it is relevant. Secondly, if the candidate declares that he does not wish to discuss the topic, his wishes must be respected, provided that he is aware of any important way in which such a refusal might prejudice his application.

Carrying a large number of rules in one's head is difficult. Many find it easier to have a simple model of the role they are playing. What the candidate wants is easily understood. Anxiously aware that his future depends on his assessor, he would like him to be God — all knowing, all forgiving and infinitely wise; able to discern the candidate's essential merit despite any superficial drawbacks. Most assessors, however, would find such a role too demanding and the few who feel at home in it do not make good assessors.

Two images which can usefully be born in mind, however, owe something to that of the school principal or headteacher and family doctor of one's youth. These are figures of authority, but in this situation the authority should not be overbearing in any way, but should depend on the interviewer's obvious confidence in what he is doing. It should be that of someone who is totally in command of the situation and totally unruffled by anything that the candidate might say. His confidence should appear such that the candidate can be controlled when necessary by the gentlest of touches.

The headteacher is the appropriate model for an assessor testing a candidate's brain-power. If the candidate is shy or ill-at-ease, he is reassured. If he becomes familiar or facetious, he is put down firmly but gently and without any obvious annoyance. The interviewer probes firmly but with understanding. Without strain he adjusts the difficulty of his questions to the quality of the candidate's replies. If the candidate is doing well, he makes his questions more demanding. Conversely, if the candidate is floundering, he makes things simpler. If the candidate is lost, he is rescued with a discreet prompt or reassurance. (It is possible to see interviewers doing the opposite. With a good candidate they will relax and enjoy the performance; a bad one they crush.) The object is to bracket the candidate's ability by exploring its boundaries — covering the ground and changing the difficulty of the questions.

The family doctor image is better fitted to the exploration of a candidate's personality. Here the candidate is encouraged to expand and talk about himself. The probing is as thorough, but the touch is gentler. If the candidate becomes irrelevant or wordy, he is controlled as firmly, but the tone is understanding. Sympathy will be forthcoming for difficulties; understanding for failures. But the assessor is in control; not by any sort of force but by the confidence of his manner and the quality of his own performance.

These images help to answer the questions that assessors sometimes ask about humour in interviews. It can have its place in an interview, building up rapport or relieving an awkward situation, but it should never be at the candidate's expense and it should be used sparingly. However much the candidate responds to a joke, the situation is a very serious one for him and in retrospect he may be very resentful of any apparent failure by an assessor to take it equally seriously.

There are those who attempt to put the candidate at ease by assuring the candidate that they, themselves, are ordinary and fallible people. The point is most probably valid; the impulse to supply reassurance praiseworthy. But the technique is generally counterproductive.

Whatever candidates may say (or imply in their manner) they want to be assessed by a figure of authority. Authority should be understanding and sympathetic. It may be genial and may share a joke, but fundamentally it is never less than totally serious about the candidate's application.

A further point is that candidates sometimes come to an interview prepared to play a role — that of the dynamic, fast-talking manager to be seen in television plays or the more familiar one of the lighthearted and somewhat feckless student. But most will respond to the interviewer's manner and a well-organised and serious approach to the interview by the interviewer will normally result in a businesslike response from the candidate.

In contrast to a sympathetic approach some organisations deliberately set out to make an interview stressful. The candidate may be treated aggressively, sneered at and in other ways made to feel uncomfortable. The reasoning behind this is obscure. In some cases it appears to be to find out if the candidate is made of the 'right stuff'. (If he gets upset, he isn't.) More legitimately, it might be supposed to reveal any weak points he might have or to test his resistance to stress. Such an approach is less popular than it was and for the best of reasons — it doesn't work.

Follow-up research has established that reactions to such treatment do not test resistance to stress — the candidate's response is specific to that situation and does not predict his responses in any wider way. Further, once such an approach is known to be used, it becomes a ritual for which the candidate is prepared and any value it might have has been lost.

More seriously such an approach destroys the rapport and the candidate becomes guarded and careful in his replies for the rest of the interview. Experts who recommend a courteous approach are not moralising. Courtesy gets better results.

Techniques of questioning

In a general sense this entire book is as much concerned with techniques as it is with the matter of an interview. Here the term is taken in a narrower sense. It is concerned with ways of framing a question or series of questions.

Open and closed questions. This is a useful distinction. Closed questions are those which ask for a brief, defined answer — 'yes','no' or something equally limited. These have their uses. If a year is not accounted for on an application form, an assessor will want to ask why. Generally, the answer will be brief; the candidate was unemployed or simply made a mistake in filling the form in. If his writing is indistinct, it might be necessary to ask, for example, if his age has been correctly read. But generally such questions are an inefficient way of finding out about the candidate. The objective is to ask open-ended questions which can be answered in different ways and allow the candidate to expand on a subject. Overall, the assessor aims to say as little as possible in proportion to the candidate. Thus the sort of question to ask is not 'Did you play football' at school?', but 'What sport do you play?' or 'What did you do at school apart from study?' In this way the candidate can be got to say a lot about himself, while the interviewer says little.

A related mistake to that of the closed question, is to ask one where the right answer is obvious. 'Are you prepared to work hard?' or 'What do you think of the government's shoddy record on housing?' Here any candidate can see what the assessor wants to hear and, if he wishes, supply the answer.

Controlling the answer. Given an open question many candidates will respond appropriately. Some, however, will be brief or laconic in their replies. In some cases, this will be due to shyness and the way to get a fuller response is to reward the answers with a show of interest. 'I see', 'That's interesting' or 'What do you think about?' may be appropriate for particular situations. If the candidate is naturally laconic, other devices may be more efficient. 'Can you give an example or two?' or 'Can you expand on that?' might meet the case. Sometimes a simple 'So?' might work. It is essential not to do what one might otherwise do instinctively, as part of normal good manners, and fill awkward gaps by talking oneself. The interviewer must concentrate on getting the candidate to speak.

On the other hand, some candidates talk too much. Some are diffuse — they talk a lot while saying little — and there is not a lot that can be done with them. If the candidate wanders from the point or answers the wrong question, he must be firmly but courteously controlled. 'Yes, but what I really wanted to know' or 'very interesting, but what I really meant was' are possible devices for this purpose.

Deciding to make an intervention of this sort is fairly easy in an intellectual discussion, but when the candidate's personality is being assessed, there are occasions when it can be very much more difficult. If a candidate is aware of an awkward patch in his history, he may approach it in easy stages or by a sort of emotional strip-tease in which the interviewer is required to show obvious approval for each step in disclosure. Handling this sort of situation is hazardous and the job is best done by a professional psychologist accustomed to handling this sort of situation. It is easy to stop the flow. It is extremely difficult to decide whether it is worthwhile to listen to a stream of apparent irrelevancies in the hope that the candidate will eventually come to a significant point. Experienced interviewers can make mistakes in this situation; beginners should not be downcast by difficulties encountered. Such difficulties are not necessarily to the candidate's discredit, as they were not in the case of one whose sister had been murdered a month or so previously. His inability to talk easily about some of his attitudes to other people was unsurprising. (The important question of when it is worth taking trouble with a difficult candidate is discussed elsewhere.)

Funnel questions. A useful technique in the interviewer's armoury is that of the funnel question. For an example, the interviewer may wish to get an estimate of a candidate's energy by finding out how he spends his spare time. It is wasteful of time to ask such questions as 'Do you play any sport?' or 'Do you read much?' Covering the necessary ground would entail going through a long list of possible activities.

The efficient way is to begin with the broadest possible question. 'How do you spend your time when you are not working?' (This is preferable to 'How do you spend your spare time?', which the candidate might take to exclude activities such as voluntary work in hospital, which are not always counted as spare time.) The answer can be classified under various headings such as sport, social, cultural and so on and each of these explored in turn. Having found out that the candidate plays football in winter and tennis in summer, the interviewer can go on to find out how much time and effort he puts into these activities. By beginning with the broadest possible question, the interviewer ensures that no activity is missed. Funnelling down to the detailed question he gets the right overall picture.

Reflecting questions. Sometimes a candidate's answer will be unclear. Sometimes the right thing is to say so. Sometimes it is more useful — especially if the candidate appears to be having difficulty — to rephrase his answer and ask him if he has been understood correctly: 'Are you saying that we cannot afford a Star Wars programme?' or 'Is your point that the real answer to crime is better policing?'

Sometimes the candidate's difficulty can be emotional rather than intellectual. Some people are not accustomed to talk about their feelings and find it difficult to do so. They are often relieved and grateful for a little discreet help. 'Are you saying that you are a shy person?' or 'Did you keep quiet because you were embarrassed?' are the kind of question that can help a candidate past a difficult spot. The interrogative form is not always necessary. 'That must have been frightening' or 'A lot of people would find that worrying' may help the candidate with his account.

Testing breadth of view. It is important that a manager should be able to see that there can be different points of view on most subjects and to understand views opposed to their own. It is important to test that they can do this. Blunt contradiction of a point of view that the candidate has expressed is unconstructive and may introduce a feeling of conflict. The productive technique involves making the point impersonally. 'But some people would say that the unions have a case' or 'One point of view is that ...'.

An alternative method — which has saved many an interviewer from drying up in embarrassed silence — is simply to ask, 'What is the case for the opposite point of view?' This is a useful and economic way of doing the job.

Taking Notes. Most interviewers will want to take some notes and will have their own views on what should be recorded. Items which it is useful to take down include details missing from the application form, explanations of puzzles arising from the form or any other source or any point where the exact details are likely to be challenged by other assessors. Tact is as necessary here as at any other point. If the candidate is clearly embarrassed at any point, he does not want to see the interviewer scribbling away. The best thing to do is to lay one's pen down and memorise the details for recording at a later stage.

These then are some of the techniques which an assessor will have at his command. The resourceful assessor, as he gains in experience, will acquire and develop a collection of such devices.

Content

Whether an interview is part of a selection process or the entire selection process in itself, it is essentially the middle stage of a three-stage process. These are preparation, interview and assessment. It is a sad and observable fact that, even where the interview itself is done well, the other two stages are often badly neglected.

The simple fact is that an interview needs planning. An assessor should first study the available information — application form, references and the like. These may raise questions and will certainly leave gaps. The interviewer must decide what he needs to learn about the candidate. 'Is he clever enough?', 'Is his professional knowledge adequate?', 'Can he explain a complicated technical point clearly to a layman?' or 'Is he energetic and enterprising enough?' are queries that might arise. Knowing what he needs to know about the candidate and the time available for interview he can then decide what must be tested, what will probably have to be taken for granted and what might be investigated if time allows.

The assessor may want an overall view of the candidate and he will probably have a standard format for an interview covering the qualities required, which he will then adjust to meet the needs of individual candidates.

Whatever the method adopted, the interviewer should begin an interview with a list of questions that need to be answered — a set of hypotheses to be investigated. A referee, for example, drops a hint that a candidate may not be a reliable worker. One therefore needs to go into his record to see if this hint can be substantiated or dismissed. A candidate's application form may show a blank year. Is this a mistake in arithmetic? Is something being concealed? If so, what?

At the same time an assessor has to be prepared to be flexible as the interview develops. The candidate may drop hints, wittingly or otherwise, of topics that should be investigated further. He may make assertions that should be questioned, or reveal gaps in what one thought one knew about him. An assessor therefore has to maintain a balance between his prepared scheme and the necessity to respond to the candidate's account of himself as it develops.

Of course, the candidate is not simply giving a factual account of himself. Generally most candidates are trying to represent themselves in a favourable light. They will present evidence that is to their credit and leave out things which they think will do them no good. This means that the interviewer will not only listen to what is being said but will be alive to what is not being said — what is being avoided or omitted — and bring it into the discussion.

In all this, of course, the candidate's account must not be taken at its face value. People vary greatly in their self-esteem and while this is a factor to be evaluated it must not be allowed to colour one's judgement of the other factors. At one extreme is the candidate who described a week at a holiday camp 60 miles from home as a great achievement in organisation and enterprise. At the other was the candidate who hitch-hiked from London to within 100 miles of the source of the Niger and regarded his failure to cover this last 100 miles as serious evidence of personal weakness. His assessors, needless to say, took a different view.

In another case, a candidate had been working as a tax-collector. Asked if he had had any problems, he said no. The interviewer was about to pass on, but decided to press the question. The British were, he said, a law-abiding nation but he found it difficult to believe that everyone paid up without protest. Oh well, the candidate replied, a lot of people shouted at him and one farmer had set his dogs on him, so that he had had to run for his life, but no, he hadn't had any problems. ('This candidate', the interviewer wrote, 'has an optimistic outlook and is inclined to make light of difficulties.')

More basically, candidates vary in truthfulness. Some are completely open and frank, some are clearly untruthful and untrustworthy. But such candidates form a very small fraction of those one is likely to see. Most candidates are surprisingly open and truthful about themselves. In part, they act in the belief that they do not want a job for which they are not qualified and that the assessors are better qualified than they are to judge this. (An interview for promotion is, of course, a different situation.) In conflict with this, they also seek to impress. The great majority of candidates are at times telling the truth as they see it and at others what they believe their assessors want to hear. This is entirely comprehensible and is no reflection on their integrity. But it does mean that the assessors have to distinguish one approach from the other and where appropriate, guide the candidate back into more profitable exchanges.

Generally, any statement made by a candidate may be regarded as the opening move in a long exchange. Alternatively, the interviewer may decide to accept it and move on. But the decision is the interviewer's and not the candidate's. The interviewer must be aware that facts may be capable of several interpretations. It is the interviewer's job to continue the questioning until the right interpretation has been established. The information that a candidate has changed jobs many times, for example, may be evidence that:

1. He is a natural job hopper and not to be relied on.
2. He has an immature attitude to work and unrealistic expectations which are naturally disappointed in any job he takes.
3. He is a person of unusual drive and courage who has not hesitated to change when he saw a better opportunity to make use of his talents.

4. He has had bad luck with jobs. The realistic expectations he had formed were disappointed.
5. There is something about his personality that means he cannot work in a team and has therefore had to move on.
6. He has slowly been gaining in the knowledge of his own abilities and will now show a more mature approach.
7. He has been outstandingly successful and because of his high reputation has had a series of offers he could not refuse.
8. The jobs were only meant to be temporary or were short-term fixed contract.
9. He has little sense of obligation to others.

The reader may well think of other explanations and those suggested are not necessarily distinct. The essential point is that it is the interviewer's responsibility to establish which are the valid reasons, to be clear how far they count in the candidate's favour and how far against.

Arbitrary decisions and insights should not be accepted. The assessor who declared that, because a candidate had resigned his commission in the Army and had been divorced, he was not a person to be trusted, was not doing an acceptable job. Clearly there were many alternative explanations to be explored and some of them might well have been to the candidate's credit. The essential need, in every case, is to establish the facts of a situation before reaching a judgement about the candidate's personality.

A feature of candidates' discourse is that they will generally describe their behaviour in terms of the situations they found themselves in. One will say, for example that he took a particular course because it was an easy option or decided to stop a journey at a particular point because it became too difficult. The interviewer assessing these situations is trying to come up with explanations of the candidates' conduct in terms of their personalities. He will try out, for example, the explanation that they are looking for soft options. This would fit the case given, but further exploration might lead to the conclusion that they are normally prudent or have a self-mocking sense of humour or some such. It is vital to get accounts of enough incidents and decisions to be confident that a stable feature of their personality has been identified. (Candidates who account for their behaviour in such a way — by describing themselves as resolute, determined and the like should be gently but firmly dissuaded from doing so. People who do this are rare.)

One serious drawback of interviews or any assessment

procedures, even those that last for several days is that they do not give much direct information on vital aspects of personality such as energy, drive, reliability and the like. It is easy to be misled by what one does see. The way in which these characteristics may be assessed will be discussed in the next chapter. The point for the moment is to avoid putting too much weight on immediate impressions. This is a serious and sometimes fatal cause of error.

Finally, it must be recorded that interviewing is never totally reliable. Even the best interviewers can make fundamental mistakes. It is possible for two equally good interviewers to get different responses from the same candidates. One can never guarantee complete reliability. The best one can do is to minimise the unreliability of the method.

However well an assessor interviews, he never completely eliminates his personality from the exchanges. The candidates are responding to this, and their responses will be coloured by it. Jolly interviewers frequently report that the interviewee is a jolly chap. And the writer remembers, without affection, the assessor who found the majority of his candidates dull. It was easy to see why. The best interviewers are aware of the influence their own approach has on the interviewee and are able to make the necessary adjustments for this.

Panel or serial interviews?

There have been attempts to establish by experiment whether, when there is more than one interviewer, it is more profitable to combine them to see the candidate as a panel or whether it is more efficient for them to interview the candidate alone and in turn. Such attempts have yielded ambiguous results, but it is not clear that they could provide a useful answer. Experience suggests that everything depends on the individual assessors involved.

A panel or board interview means that as each member puts his questions in turn, the other members are free to put a different interpretation on the candidate's answer and possibly on the question itself. In this way there is a check on the person interviewing and possibly fresh insights into the candidate and his responses. This means that the method is useful for interviewers who lack experience and for this, or any other reason, lack confidence in each other. In these situations, however, great demands may be made on the chairman of the panel in getting each member to make a useful contribution or alternatively in keeping the peace.

For a professional team, who do have confidence in each other's way of working, there are great advantages in a series of interviews where each assessor sees each candidate alone and with an agreed area of assessment to cover. Firstly, there is the mechanical point that the time spent interviewing can be increased without extra cost. For example, if each interview lasts half an hour and three interviewers are involved, the candidate is seen for an hour and a half. With the assessors combined on a panel the candidate is seen for only half an hour.

A second advantage is that it is easier to build up rapport with an individual interviewer than a committee so that the candidate will talk more freely. This makes greater demands on the individual interviewer because a candidate may present a different side of his personality at different interviews.

But with experienced interviewers any such variation can be used to enhance the overall view of the candidate. Such assessors will be mature enough to know that the candidate may respond in different ways to different kinds of interview and interviewer and that their pooled experience can lead to a better all-round understanding of the candidate's personality.

In a typical instance, an assessor with the job of assessing a candidate's intellect reported that he was very reserved. A second assessor, on inviting him to talk about himself as a person, found him gushing. The third assessor was told by the candidate that he felt apprehensive in his first interview and that he had consequently over-reacted to the friendliness of the second interviewer. These comments led to an assessment that was clearly more valid than any that could have been derived from any single interview.

Post-selection interviews

For a particularly critical appointment it can be sensible to ask the recommended candidate to discuss the strategy of the organisation, the part he is to play and the scope he will have for his own ideas before the final appointment is made. If it later turns out that there is a significant misunderstanding in any of these areas it can be very upsetting and expensive for both parties. A post-selection interview, in which someone who has been assessed as suitable for the organisation can decide if the organisation suits him, has obvious advantages. He can then ask questions which he might have avoided during the selection process for fear that they might prejudice his chances of success and the firm's objectives and problems can be discussed more comfortably and at a length that would be uneconomic at the selection stage.

Special indications of personality

Claims are made that a great deal can be learned about someone's personality by observing some limited feature of it. Handwriting and body posture are often advanced as such highly revealing features. Astrology also has its supporters and there are those who claim that a study of a person's hands or features can be deeply revealing.

One can readily agree that a person's handwriting shows something about him. So too will the ties he wears or the condition in which he keeps his shoes. But the suggestion that such a restricted area of observation can provide an accurate guide to wide areas of a person's behaviour is implausible. To accept such a claim would require a large scale revision of our normal ideas of the way in which people should be assessed. We would, most of us, be prepared to consider the view that we have been mistaken. But we could not responsibly do so without strong evidence that these special indications were both useful and valid. While large claims are made, there is no respectable evidence that any of these methods are valid.

Until such evidence is produced any deductions made by these methods can only be regarded as clues. At best they are a starting point for investigation rather than facts to be used in reaching a verdict.

Eye contact

The oldest and the most enduring of beliefs about body language concerns eye contact. This is simply that a person who is honest will look you in the eye when speaking to you. Someone who does not is shifty and unreliable. This belief should have been scrapped long ago, but it still persists. One must first note that this is a Western legend — it is accepted in Europe and the USA, but not in Africa. Further, in Thailand it is considered extremely rude to look people in the eye. One might on these grounds alone have doubts about the validity of the legend.

These doubts have been fully confirmed by the investigators who have observed what people actually do with their eyes when talking to each other. Eye movement can be exceedingly complex but the rough rule is that when we are talking to people we look at them. When we are uncertain of what we want to say we break eye contact because this makes it easier to think. When we listen to people we demonstrate that we are doing so by looking at them, but again we will break contact if we want to think. The most likely reason for a person dropping his gaze when you are speaking to him is that he wishes to think about what you are saying. There are other reasons. People may break eye contact because they find it embarrassing. They may be embarrassed because they feel guilty. They may feel guilty because they have something to feel guilty about. They may feel guilty about being dishonest. So there is just a trace of truth in the legend, but this is far too slight to make this anything like a reliable test. But some people will look you steadily in the eye. What does this mean? There are two likely explanations. The first is that the unfortunate person concerned has some sort of eye trouble. Possibly he is grossly shortsighted and can only see you as a confused blur. Secondly, in some sense of the word, he may be a confidence man. Because we have the legend of the manly handshake and the direct gaze, people who wish to impress us as honest practice these accomplishments. One should not be impressed with their success.

It is worth remembering that many dishonest people feel no guilt about their dishonesty, and that many who feel guilty have no more than most of us to feel guilty about. They may, in fact, be people with high standards which they feel they never quite meet and they may be unusually conscientious and reliable.

Summary

This section has emphasised the need for interviewers to begin with a clear idea of what they are attempting to assess and the need for the right manner and technique in assessing it. Having decided what they want to know, assessors should get the candidate to talk as freely as possible, intervening only to ask a new question or to guide the candidate back to relevance, when he has gone astray. The relative advantages of panel and serial interviews have been discussed and some beliefs about special indicators of personality have been placed in context.

4.3 Beyond the interview

Minimal selection

Successful interviewing is demanding in time and resources. For this reason some organisations do not attempt to do the job thoroughly. A large retail chain, for example, took on a lot of trainees after a brief check on their suitability. Selection appeared to be cheap and unfussy. But at the end of the year over 95% had left. This meant that the real selection procedure had been spread over the year and so had turned out to be very expensive. The firm concerned decided to spend money on improving its initial selection.

Such a tactic is not always wrong. The armed services rely greatly on the personal qualities of their officers and these cannot be tested with the right degree of thoroughness in a brief procedure. While the initial selection is careful, it is to choose those who appear suitable for training. The training itself provides an important part of the total selection procedure. And firms of accountants, for example, get a lot of basic work done cheaply by taking on more people as trainees than they will employ permanently.

There are other views of the way in which to get the right person for the job at minimal expense. One now lost in the mists of history — where it was in any case of limited applicability — is that you simply offered people a job and then told them how you wanted it done. It is still possible for a consultant to find managers who regret that sound working practices will not be possible until this approach has been reinstated.

Such an approach will not be found in present-day management theorising, but one related to it has its advocates. On this view, people joining an organisation undergo a process of acculturalisation. More simply they have to learn the rules — written and unwritten — which govern the organisation, to perform well within it. There is obviously something in this. Bishops, civil servants, judges, advertising men and managers have to learn the customs and ways of speech of the organisations they join. However, to most of us, this is obviously a limited part of the job requirements. For any job, a person must be clever enough and a person cannot make himself cleverer. To get business done, a person must have the right degree of energy and staying power and there is no known method of increasing these qualities.

One version of this general approach points out that people have a self-image — a picture of themselves in which they are dynamic, outgoing or reflective or whatever. The task of selection is then that of matching the self-image of the applicant with the culture of the organisation. Selection thus becomes a process akin to courtship, in which the applicant and organisation reveal themselves to each other and finally reach a mutual decision on whether the applicant should join.

The objections to this approach are obvious. Many people have an inaccurate or superficial image of themselves. And a successful organisation must recognise its images for what they are and be prepared to assess more fundamental qualities. But, even more to the point, few of us could accept that people are as plastic as these theories require. People, most of us believe, are fixed between certain limits and it follows that the job of selection must be to find out what these limits are.

Further, the approach has some unacceptably chilling implications. It implies that individuality in a member of an organisation is undesirable or impermissible — in the terms of the Japanese proverb, 'The nail that sticks out must be knocked in.' Western society has taken a different view and while there can be few who have escaped some painful adaptation to the demands of the job, there is a strong belief that organisations need the stimulus that people can make as individuals.

The last few paragraphs have been something of a diversion. Few would deny the desirability of selection, but there are those who deny that it is possible. Assessors are bound to make mistakes, so that the attempt is not worth making. But this is to slide from the fact that we must sometimes make mistakes — which is unchallengeable — to the position that we must always make them — which is self-evidently untenable.

The basic arguments about the approach to be adopted by a particular organisation should not be in terms so much of feasibility, but in terms of economics — more precisely in terms of cost-effectiveness. Selection costs money. But so does recruiting the wrong people. There is no need to catalogue the ways in which an unsuitable manager may fail to earn his keep or disrupt the organisation. Given that this manual is largely concerned with people who are expensive to employ and will have a significant effect on the efficiency of the organisation, there is obviously a powerful argument for making selection as efficient as possible.

Minimising mistakes at this stage should minimise the overall expense of employing people. And minimising mistakes entails using an assessment centre.

Assessment centres

Assessment centres are generally accepted as the most efficient method of selection and appraisal. It is unfortunate that they should have been invested with a mystique which is off-putting to candidates and embarrassing to organisers. This is doubly unfortunate when the workings of such a system are manifestly rational and, in historical retrospect, rather obvious.

Such centres have theoretical roots in the U.S., Great Britain and Germany, but undoubtedly the ancestor of all is the War Office Selection Board system (WOSB) devised by the British Army for the selection of officers in the early 1940s. The early disasters of the war made it obvious that selection of officers was inefficient and that a more rigorous system was needed. WOSB's undoubted success has led to the wide use of similar systems in many countries.

Civilian use began immediately after the war with a number of organisations in the U.K., but of these only the Civil Service Selection Board (CSSB) survived continuously until the present day. In the U.S.A., the first civilian assessment centre was set up by the Bell Telephone Company in 1955 and has been widely copied throughout the world and has been re-exported to the U.K.

The design of assessment centres varies in detail, but all have some essential features in common.

1. The objective is to assess the candidate as a whole person — covering all his qualities — unlike simpler procedures which may rely, for example, on a trade test plus a simple interview.

2. The qualities required are defined by an analysis of the job (or the series of jobs making up a career).

3. The selection uses a number of techniques — intelligence tests, interviews, group exercises and other job simulations. Of these, the job simulations are the methods which are most closely identified with the assessment centre procedure in popular understanding. Few have not heard of the practical tests, used in WOSB — crossing obstacles, carrying heavy boxes, jumping ditches, climbing nets and the like. In the immediate post-war years, it dawned on people that these were not really appropriate

tests for top managers and more relevant tests were introduced. The in-basket exercise is probably the most widely known. Typically, this simulates a situation where the candidate arrives to take up a new job and finds a note from his secretary saying that she will be away and that his predecessor is not available. She has left him an unsorted basket of letters, memos and reports which he must deal with in a limited time. Some documents call for no more than initialling to show that he has read them. Some call for careful thought and a reasoned reply or recommendation. The candidate's response may be discussed further at a follow-up interview. In other organisations candidates have to analyse a single large scale problem and produce a reasoned solution.

Such tests can give a good prediction of management success. One authority is widely quoted as having remarked that their face validity is 'almost frighteningly high'. This is literally true of one of the earliest known examples, the selection of *'arditi'* by the Italian Army in the First World War. Candidates had, *inter alia*, to run through a machine-gun barrage in which wounds were actually inflicted. The follow-up studies which modern practice regards as essential do not appear to have been carried out, but it would be a very hard-line purist who denied successful candidates their right to the title of 'men of daring'. Present day tests do not achieve the same degree of realism but they are carefully designed to represent the job as closely as possible.

4. Candidates are assessed in groups as part of the procedure. The armed services use physical tests of various kinds, the British Civil Service uses a simulated committee and other organisations simulate groups relevant to their work.

The groups may be leaderless or the members may take it in turns to be chairmen. Most organisations use both. In a leaderless group, it is easier to see what sort of influence individual members can exert and how they relate to others. Where there is a designated leader, assessors get more direct evidence of his ability to perform in that role.

Such groups should contain from four to eight candidates, the number chosen depending on the test procedure used and the assessors available. Such exercises are highly realistic and groups can develop a strong identity. At least one marriage has resulted from people who first met in this way.

5. There is a team of assessors, so that the judgement of one is subject to check by the others. All will share responsibility for the final assessment of the candidate, but each will give particularly

close attention to certain aspects. There are at least three natural roles for these assessors.

The first is that of the young manager or rising star. This would be a person a couple of grades above the entry level or with about ten years experience of the job. (Neither measure is intended to be precise.) Generally, such people are good at testing a candidate's intellectual quality — his ability to present a case, defend it, argue and persuade. Being engaged in current management, they are well qualified to represent the current requirements of their organisation.

Used alone they tend, again in general, to have some disadvantages. They have a natural tendency, which will be more powerful if it is not recognised, to see candidates as rivals — to be defeated in argument. This they can be trained out of, but because of their relatively limited experience, they tend to be less good at assessing personal qualities and seeing how different kinds of people can fit into the organisation. This comes more naturally to other kinds of assessor.

One is best described as an elder statesman — a senior and possibly retired manager with a wide experience of working life. Outstandingly successful people are not necessarily the best in this job. Someone who has encountered failures and disappointments along the way may have developed a better understanding of how people cope with such experiences. And overall such an assessor should bring wisdom and maturity to the team. He is also naturally qualified for the job of chairman of the assessing team.

Judgements of potential for growth and the more difficult aspects of personality are most reliably carried out by a psychologist trained for this sort of work. He is equipped with techniques to get the best out of candidates who other assessors might find difficult, with theories that enable him to make sense of his observations and, also very important, should be free from the unconscious theories which can lead the unwary into error. He is also able to relate the results of intelligence and other tests to the overall judgement of the candidate. A good psychologist can improve the quality of a panel's assessment of the more difficult aspects of a candidate's personality; the more so with difficult candidates.

Psychologists can be expensive or in short supply. Some centres, for this reason, prefer not to use them in an assessing team, but to keep them on hand as advisor to a number of such teams. The Royal Navy used women officers as substitutes for the job during the Second World War and has continued to do so to its own satisfaction.

The uses of centres

Assessment centres are used in two ways. The first is for the selection of new entrants into an organisation. Such selection is among the most vital investment decisions an organisation has to make and the expense of the procedure is seen to be justified when weighed against the cost resulting from selecting unsuitable people or from missing suitable ones. This point is particularly important when seen in conjunction with the fact that the best people are not always easily spotted at the selection stage. At this stage the candidates' record of achievement is slight and much of the information about them — academic performance for example — is only obliquely relevant. For this reason full and thorough testing is necessary and the judgement of the assessors is exercised to the maximum. The need to recruit the right people is high-lighted by the surprising but established finding that anyone entering as a management trainee, in the UK, has a 70% chance of reaching top management. (This depends, of course, on their staying with the organisation and on the fact that many others do not.)

Secondly, centres are also used for the assessment of existing employees with a view to using them in more senior jobs, accelerating their progress up the hierarchy or developing their usefulness to the organisation. Importantly, the procedures are often used to find out what sort of experience or training successful candidates need to make such progress. At this stage, there is a lot more information available from the candidate's record with the organisation. Indeed it is arguable and is often argued that such assessment is unnecessary if a proper reporting system exists. To this apparently reasonable point of view there are two important objections. Firstly, given the realities of reporting — different standards among report writers, their possibly limited understanding of what higher management involves and the different relationships with the supervised — an assessment centre that ensures that common standards are applied to all candidates will be more efficient.

Further, assessment centre methods are best used when the jobs for which the candidates are being assessed are significantly different from those they are doing. There is not much point in using such an expensive method for a simple promotion to the next grade of management. But when, for example, a chemist or a salesman is being considered for transfer to management, then qualities that they will have had little or no opportunity to demonstrate must be assessed and such assessment is best done by the centre approach. To make the point in another way, the more assessment is concerned with an individual's potential than his present performance, the more the centre approach will pay off in terms of enhanced efficiency. Nevertheless, when a centre is used for the assessment of existing staff it does have the advantage of a more relevant track record to work on and it is also helped by the fact that candidates have a better understanding of the organisation and the jobs they are applying for.

Difficulties

There are some immediately obvious difficulties. The most obvious is that centres are expensive and the expense involved is much more visible than that which arises from selecting unsuitable candidates. Anyone attempting to set up such a centre should make an ally of an accountant who can give a firm estimate of the cost of such failures.

A small firm could not contemplate such expense, but an unsuitable appointment can be much more serious than for a large organisation which can afford to tuck some of its failures away in places where they can do no harm. The obvious way out is to use a consultant, but choosing the right consultants might not be easy. The old slogan that 'you only get what you pay for' is no more accurate here than for any other buying decision. It is possible to pay a lot for very little.

But there are less obvious difficulties. While potential entrants are, with the rarest of exceptions, respectful towards the procedure and are happy to work on the assumption that the assessors know their jobs, internal candidates can be very resentful of such assessment. In part, this may be inevitable. They are committed to the organisation in a way in which outsiders — who are generally confident of getting other job offers if they are successful or not — will not be. Failure for them will be much more significant and can lead to the loss of the ambitions with which they entered the organisation.

This means that care has to be taken in explaining the aims of the assessment. Such explanation must be based on a sympathetic understanding of the candidates' fears and a realisation that these may not be rationally or directly expressed. A passionate protest that the candidates' record should be the deciding factor can only be answered in part by a rational explanation of the need to test potential for novel tasks. Such a protest may mask a deeper fear that the organisation has unexplained or even sinister motives for assessing them. Alternatively objectors may fear that they are being tested for irrelevant social graces or that their points of relative weakness will be given undue weight.

Such resentments must be handled in two ways. Firstly, the aims of assessment must be frankly stated and the relevance of the procedure must be justified. Frankness is indispensable. If the stated aim is to determine training needs but those who do well are promoted while the others are not, resentment is only to be expected. It may be less necessary to justify the procedure, but the organisers and assessors must be prepared to do so if required.

Secondly, a counselling service for unsuccessful members of the organisation is necessary. It is often possible to point out that they can still expect a rewarding career or go up the ladder if by a slower route. In any case the opportunity to let off emotional steam with a sympathetic listener should be built into an efficient system. The Royal Air Force, which has to turn down over 90% of applicants for training as a pilot, is particularly good at such counselling.

Incidental benefits

A well run assessment centre has some useful incidental benefits. Firstly, people place a higher value on a job that they have got after thorough testing than on one which has been easily obtained. Secondly, candidates will be sceptical of advertised claims to efficiency to some degree and a selection process that is manifestly thorough and well organised provides powerful support to such a claim.

Thirdly, the procedure will use working managers from different parts of the organisation. Their experience stimulates an interest in assessment and provides them with assessment skills that will be useful in other parts of the organisation. At the same time such participation avoids the danger, to which selection is otherwise prone, of being apparently divorced from the working part of the organisation and so imposing recruits on managers without properly understanding their requirements. A belief on the managers' part that recruits are unsuitable can too easily be self-fulfilling if they do not give them the attention and guidance they need in starting a new job. And such failures may be attributed to poor selection.

Improving the system

Research into the efficiency of assessment centres — the degree to which they predict both long and short term performance as managers — has yielded some clear-cut results.

They have confirmed the user's belief that a well-run centre — that is one with experienced organisers, well designed tests and assessors who are skilled and trained — can produce better results than any other approach. Importantly, it has established that predictions become more valid as the manager gains in experience than they are for his early years. This means that an organisation which wishes to reduce error to the minimum and is prepared to pay to do so, should adopt such a procedure.

But this finding offers no guarantee that any procedure that follows an assessment centre type programme will yield the same sort of results. It is relatively easy to reproduce the mechanics of a successful procedure. These are well-known and have been widely discussed. Indeed suggestions for improving the procedures have been largely in terms of methods.

This, unfortunately, has obscured the way in which improvement can be achieved. This is indicated by follow-up studies which have demonstrated what to many people will be an obvious point, namely that the performance of people under test is not always representative of the way they will do the job. Some may do better than at the assessment stage. There, they may do less well because the experience is novel or because they have not developed the skills of self-presentation or simply because being observed is disconcerting, especially to those who are uncertain of what is being looked for. On appointment the shy blossom, the awkward can quickly learn how to present themselves effectively and the tense often relax.

At the same time, there are those who may perform better under test than on the job. There are those who respond to the stimulus of the situation and the interest of their assessors, but who, when left to work on their own, quickly become bored and uninterested.

Further, management is a complex activity and job simulation tests are artificial to a degree which may be significant for some candidates. In particular, time scales are compressed — problems that would normally be considered for days, weeks, months or even years have to be solved in an hour or two. And in real life the problems would be tackled by managers with a lot of background knowledge of the organisation, its approach, customers, markets and the like. When the candidate is someone about to graduate from a university with no work experience, assessors have to be able to identify some basic qualities as distinct from specific know-how and pure tests of these qualities which allow for lack of any previous experience are not possible, leaving those with such experience at an advantage. Important qualities such as drive, determination, reliability and capacity for growth are not immediately observable but must be estimated in other ways by skilled assessors.

Statistical analysis has demonstrated what will seem obvious to observers of the process — that is that the judgement of the assessors is a vital factor at every stage of the assessment. This is true for intelligence tests as much as any other stage. Often referred to as objective tests, they cease to be so when applied to the practical business of assessment, as this involves interpreting them in relation to the individual candidates' personalities.

This finding has implications of the greatest practical importance. It means that an assessment centre procedure must be regarded as providing a framework which gives the maximum help to the exercise of the assessors' judgement. If there has been a significant development in the use of such centres in recent years it has been a growth in humility. There was a time when the method appeared paramount. Its users were certainly entitled to regard it as superior to an everyday selection interview. Its face validity — to use the self-explanatory technical term — is high. However, once it is appreciated that assessors are themselves human and necessarily suffer from the limitations inseparable from that condition, the situation can be seen to be more complicated. This book was written in the light of such an understanding and to provide practical help in this situation.

The Assessors

The long term hope must be that methods will be devised that will make the procedures much less dependent on human judgement. However no such methods are in sight and this necessarily means that the quality of assessment depends critically on the quality of the assessors. This means that they, themselves, must be selected and trained and their performance must be monitored to ensure uniform and adequate standards. A fair-sized book could be written on this subject alone. The following is a brief outline of what is involved.

Assessors must, of course, have the necessary experience and be up to the intellectual standards expected from successful candidates. After that, the fundamental and indispensable quality required in an assessor is a willingness to take the job seriously as one needing and worthy of his full attention. Anyone who resents the job as being beneath him or regards it as a side-line to be worked in with more important work, is totally unsuitable.

An almost equally indispensable quality is humility. Selection is a specialised job, requiring the use of specialised techniques and the making of judgements in unusual circumstances. Anyone who is convinced that he knows everything necessary — at any stage of his career as an assessor — is unlikely to make a good assessor. Given these basic qualifications most people can be trained to make adequate assessors.

With the aid of such devices as closed circuit television, a willing assessor can be trained to be a competent interviewer. This device is a great help in dealing with the problems of tact which a manager of a selection system may face telling assessors of their shortcomings. In particular, telling someone that he is a poor interviewer involves all the hazards involved in telling someone that they have bad breath or are a bad driver. A television recording is a great help here, putting the trainee in the position of being his own critic. Specimen group exercises can also be shown to standardise the assessors' marking. In addition, the trainee assessor should be placed with an experienced group to learn the practicalities of the job.

There is, of course, a range of abilities among assessors. Some have a natural flair for the job; others can learn the job to a high standard; others never get beyond a basic competence. To see what is involved here, it is helpful to look at assessment as something taking place on two levels. The first is that of assessing the candidates' observed performance. The convenient assumption that this is representative of how the candidate will perform on the job being no longer tenable, there is the more difficult task of relating the test performance to that in real life. This involves making allowances for the effects of the procedure, assessing potential from the tests of intelligence and giving the right weight to the candidate's personality. Doing this part well requires a high level of insight and skill. There is a need for training methods that would develop these qualities, but in their absence, management has to adopt other tactics. These include grouping assessors so that the weaknesses of one assessor are compensated for by those of another. Many otherwise capable people have their blind-spots and it is important for management to know about these.

Management may decide that an assessing team has been too harsh or too easygoing in their final judgement on a particular candidate and adjust their mark accordingly. Alternatively, management may decide that the evidence the assessing group have assembled has been weighed wrongly and make a similar adjustment.

A valuable discipline is provided by getting assessors to write reports on their candidates. This requires thought in a way that filling in a rating scale does not. It forces the assessors to make out their case clearly and also can give them an insight into what they could do better in future.

The most useful discipline is provided by follow-up studies. Statistical exercises, which correlate predictions with performance are popular and the methods of producing them are well understood. These will check whether the procedure is generally successful, but they do not generally help individual assessors to improve their performance. Even more to the point, they are expensive and beyond the means of any but a large organisation.

In any case, studies which compare predictions for individual candidates with their later reports are more useful as aids to improving performance. These can be fed back to assessors to give them insight into the way in which they can improve their assessments.

Summary

This chapter has discussed some arguments for minimising selection and suggested that in practical fact they lengthen the process and make it more expensive. The nature and use of assessment centres has been outlined. It has been argued that these are essentially a way of providing the best possible framework for the exercise of assessors' judgement and that therefore the selection, training and monitoring of assessors is of the greatest importance.

5
Qualities and Characteristics

This chapter deals with the most common judgements assessors have to make. The order in which they are discussed is that of the suggested rating scale. For convenience, the chapter has been broken down into three sections. The first deals with intellectual qualities, the second with those qualities concerned with working with others and the third with personal characteristics. As a rough rule the further into the chapter, the more difficult are the qualities discussed to assess.

5.1 Intellectual Qualities

1. Penetration	7	6	5	4	3	2	1
2. Constructive Thinking	7	6	5	4	3	2	1
3. Judgement	7	6	5	4	3	2	1
4. Numeracy	7	6	5	4	3	2	1

'Intellectual' is used here as the most useful heading to cover a number of important qualities. Anglo-Saxon society — both American and British — might find the term uncongenial and has some good reasons for doing so, but it is the best term available. There are more homely terms such as 'brain-power' or 'cleverness', but they are less precise and the latter is hardly less objectionable than the original. 'Mental ability' or 'mental capacity' might be acceptable to some people, but psychologists reserve such terms as for the more abstract quality of intelligence. And for management intelligence is not enough; what is required is intelligence that can be put to practical use.

It is a recognition of this need that leads to some of the objections to the term 'intellectual'. We all know of highly intelligent people who are inadequate in the practical affairs of life. And there are, further, two objectionable stereotypes which the term is often taken to refer to.

On one common view an intellectual is someone who believes he is clever and is at no pains to hide it. Anglo-Saxon society finds this sort of bragging particularly objectionable and people who do behave in this way are likely to be unpopular and to that extent less effective members of an organisation.

Alternatively, an intellectual is a person who converts every situation — even the most practical — into a high level of abstraction. Thus current events become 'ongoing phenomena in the environment' and a strike can be represented as 'a dysfunctional state of labour relations'. The use of such pretentious phrases in day to day business amounts to no more than an irrelevant filibuster and those who are unable to tackle concrete problems in concrete terms are simply a nuisance to those dealing with practical situations.

Neither kind of person is being suggested by the use of the term. What has to be recognised is that intellectual ability — the power to analyse and judge complex situations and reach ordered decisions — is extremely important in management of any kind. Older ideas that the right sort of character, background and school were all that are necessary have proved manifestly inadequate. It is certainly possible to be clever and unsuitable for management, but there is no evidence to suggest that success without intellectual ability is at all common.

For most management jobs then quality of intellect is a vital consideration. For some jobs too much of this quality can be a handicap. A well-known study demonstrated that a high turnover of engineering work-shop apprentices was due to the recruitment of boys who were too intelligent for the job. Rejecting applicants above a certain level greatly eased the situation. But for management in general no such limit is desirable (unless one is assessing for lower management where there is no possibility of promotion).

Estimating these qualities is not easy, but, as the roughest of rules, the more intellectual the quality the easier it is to judge accurately. The reasons for this are not difficult to see. The assessor is helped by examination results, objectively marked tests and tests designed to simulate the work that a successful candidate would do. And while appearances of drive, reliability and so on can be very deceptive, a candidate cannot convincingly pretend to be cleverer than he is.

It is, however, easy to be distracted in this area of assessment. There are a great many things that one can say about a person's intellect and a great many areas one can explore. It is necessary to resist the temptation to concentrate on some particular interest. One must aim to cover the area as broadly and as precisely as possible. Sometimes assessment may be concerned with specialist skills but for general purposes it is useful to use the classification which divides intellectual qualities into three general categories — penetration, constructive thinking and judgement.

These will be considered in turn, and the evidence from which these qualities can be assessed will be discussed. In particular, the use of intelligence tests — which are designed as measures of pure intellectual ability — will be discussed. For the moment it is enough to observe that these qualities are not purely intellectual — temperament clearly exercises an influence on people's performance. Clever people can show poor or unworldly judgement. Someone may be well endowed intellectually but lack the desire to get to the roots of complex problems. So these assessments are more complex than they might appear at first sight.

Penetration

This term is an obvious and therefore fairly harmless metaphor, and one comes across others — getting to the roots, getting to the bottom of the problem and discarding the inessentials to extract the essence.

What is being looked for is the ability to identify the essentials of a problem in a mass of material. This may be large, poorly presented, badly written, inadequate or incomplete. One looks for the ability to analyse a situation and present the essential considerations in a clear and precise form.

Assessors must be aware that there will seldom be complete agreement as to what constitutes an essential point and that therefore there is a degree of subjectivity in their own judgement. They must be prepared to recognise a good case for a point even if they reject it themselves.

It should be borne in mind that these judgements are not entirely independent. A touch of imagination is needed to spell out a point that may be inadequately made in the given material or to see the implications of something presented as bare fact. Even more clearly judgement is required to decide what is essential and what is not.

These categories are not therefore completely independent. Nevertheless the ability to identify and present the central issues in a problem can be assessed.

In making such a judgement one must be aware of some possible halo effects. An aggressive manner in discussion can lead to an overestimation of the candidate's penetrative powers (which is why some people adopt such a manner). Some manners of speech — clipped or cold and remote — can give the same sort of impression. As always these additional qualities can be evaluated in their own right without confusing them with those sought. Various styles of writing can also be seductive, and one needs again to distinguish penetration from the style that enhances it.

Constructive thinking

This is the ability to look at problems in a new and constructive way, so that new and improved solutions are possible. In some cases this may involve demonstrating that previous accounts of the problems have been misleading or unprofitable. It may involve arguing that the problem was a rather different one from what was first thought.

Judgements made of this quality in selection procedures are the least accurate of those commonly made. In order to improve on this, assessors need to have a clear idea of what they are looking for. Because terms such as 'constructive','creative' or 'original' thinking are used widely for a range of activities, there is a tendency to assume that this is one fixed quality which can appear in many different ways. In this way Picasso, crossword-puzzlers, Shakespeare, code-breakers, inventors, novelists and so on all have the same quality to a different degree, and use it in different ways. Put thus precisely, the assumption is plainly absurd. In fact, the profitable way to think is in terms of more limited abilities to think creatively in different areas. It is natural enough to think that Picasso had different qualities from those of a successful code-breaker. The analogies between their skills are clear enough, but one has to think in concrete terms of what people actually do, in order to assess the qualities required accurately.

This is relatively easy to do for those engaged in advertising, scientific research or journalism, but for those engaged in general management, it is more difficult and comment tends to stray into mystical references to the need for vision.

Definition of what is needed requires a sober realisation that techniques, markets and people are changing. The speed of change in technology needs no emphasis, but it is sometimes more difficult to take in the way in which the expectations of customers and workers are also growing. But a manager, in mid or late career, who works on the assumptions that were valid when he first started work will be well on the way to becoming a problem for his organisation, if he is not so already. The essential quality is that of being able to see the new forms which the basic problems of management develop. And, of course, there may always be ways of doing existing things better.

The manager of a work-force containing a significant proportion of a racial minority will need the imagination to see things their way and to get them to do things his way. Those working abroad will need some of the same ability and in some countries will need a great deal more. The same is true for those opening new markets in any part of the world.

All this means that a management career will present the individual with a series of novel problems which he must recognise and think through if he is to survive and prosper. At the selection stage it is possible to identify some people who are rigid and inflexible in their thinking, but thinking further and more positively about what we are looking for is difficult. This stems from the nature of thinking itself. This presents problems both to assessors and to candidates. Despite everyday experience to the contrary it is widely held that original thinking should be straightforward and clear. The simple fact is that original thinking is confused and uncertain. This is something that we all know. The puzzle is why we should feel so strongly compelled to think otherwise. Some explanation of this is given in Appendix I. The point that results is that, because hitting on an idea, refining it and presenting it in a publicly acceptable form takes a considerable time, we cannot test this entire process within the scale of any sound testing procedure. What we can hope to test is the ability to produce the raw material from which such a finished product can be developed.

This means that judgement and creative thinking cannot be assessed at the same time. If the latter is particularly important, then one has to put the candidate in a situation where he can be confident that his judgement is not also being assessed. Any reasonably informed candidate knows that judgement is a vital quality and will be reluctant to imperil his chances by making public ideas that may cast doubt on his own.

The reader will know that many organisations which set out to produce novel solutions to problems set up a situation where people are encouraged to produce ideas quite regardless of their merit ('brain-storming sessions'). Setting up this sort of situation within any assessment procedure is clearly difficult and, in any brief procedure, impossible. We are therefore normally dependent on other sources for this assessment. Of course, if we are assessing a scientist with a clear record of creative research, or a journalist with a portfolio of published work, we are in a comfortable position to make this assessment. Otherwise we are heavily dependent on references — which do not often mention this quality — or internal reports.

Judgement

There are those who regard this quality as the vital quality which marks out the high flyer from the merely competent. The idea of one vital quality — as opposed to a number of qualities in the right balance — is not supported in this manual, but there can be no doubt of its importance. We are here talking of the ability to distinguish between the central issues and the less important ones. We are also looking for a practical sense of what is workable and an understanding that what is desirable, simple or systematic is not acceptable for these reasons alone. And, further, we are looking for the ability to distance a decision from personal preferences and feelings.

This, of course, describes the qualities as related to a generalist. For professional appointments we need to assess professional judgement and adapt this general description in terms of professional criteria.

In making such assessments the assessor must, of course, be aware that judgement is to some extent a subjective quality and be prepared to treat judgements which he does not immediately accept with the respect with which he treats those of colleagues in working life. He must be prepared to recognise the soundly argued case even if some of the premises might not be those one would use himself. He also needs to separate this intellectual quality from some of its more cosmetic accompaniments. One should not be over-impressed by a candidate's presence or persuasiveness in this context. And one should recognise the sensible person who, for example, is not expressing himself well or with confidence.

One must, as in all cases, assess the performance one sees, but at the same time form an estimate of the likelihood of improvement. Judgement can be taught. An intelligent recruit can learn quickly on appointment, and will find many implicit guidelines and much explicit advice available.

In this context the assessor needs to identify those who are unlikely to learn. He can identify people who are perverse in their attitudes, egocentric in their view of the world, insensitive to the views of others or capricious and unstable in their attitudes. Such people are unlikely to acquire good judgement. Otherwise we can generally be confident that this quality can be learned. It is always rewarding to find a young candidate with a finely honed judgement, but given a candidate who is both sensible and intelligent it is often possible to predict that he can acquire it.

As a final comment it must be said that statistical analysis shows an uncomfortably high correlation between liking a person and making a favourable assessment of his judgement. There is a natural tendency to do this and it must be resisted. On the other hand thinking well of a person's judgement is a good reason for liking him.

Numeracy

Numeracy has two components. One is the ability to handle figures in a mathematical way. There is only a limited need for this among managers, particularly when calculators and computers are so widely available. For some specialist jobs — actuary or operational research scientist — mathematical knowledge is necessary and is then easily tested.

The second ability is that of being able to relate figures to the real world; to look, for example, at a set of accounts and deduce a company's prospects or to read through statistics of family structure and expenditure and identify growing markets. A list of possible activities would be large, but they are becoming increasingly important.

The skills required are not limited to scrutiny of existing data. They require also the ability to see what kinds of figures might be useful to an organisation and an ability to present data in a way that makes it readily intelligible. These activities may require a knowledge of the logic of statistical inference.

For other professions, the skills needed may require more

careful definition in the light of individual job descriptions. There will be different requirements for accountants, actuaries, computer programmers and systems analysts. Once the work to be done has been precisely defined, tests of these skills may be readily devised.

Sources of evidence

Evidence of intellectual ability can be derived from many sources which need to be weighed against each other. Some are direct — from interviews and various sorts of test. Others are indirect — examinations, references and service reports. These latter are generally available before assessment starts so at the very least they must be examined as a source of hypotheses about the candidate's strengths and weaknesses to be tested during the procedure.

Given that references tend to be on the benevolent side, it is unsafe to put much weight on them, except on the rare occasion when the referee is someone of known standards. But any negative points must be taken as something which must be carefully tested, since these are less common, and are only likely to be made if there are strong reasons for doing so. With internal staff reports one is naturally predisposed to give more weight to the comments. But these may be in relation to a lower grade job or a specialised one. One therefore has first to ask how relevant such comments can be, and how well the report writer knows the job for which the candidate is being tested. Sometimes the answers to these questions suggest that the report is of low value.

University examination results need some thinking about. Common sense suggests that they provide evidence of a candidate's ability to analyse, digest and reproduce information at a fairly advanced level. Some thought must be given to the subject involved. For professional appointments the subject is clearly important. For generalists it is much less so, although one would expect differences in ability from those who have read different subjects. A graduate in one of the numerate disciplines should be strong in this respect but might lack recent experience of writing. The assessor might therefore look more for potential than polish in this area. He would make no such allowances for an historian or someone with a degree in English, but provided they had the basic abilities he could make allowances for those less practised in numerical work. In weighing such results an assessor has to remember that the quality of teaching a candidate receives can affect the result quite markedly. Where it is clear that this has been either strong or weak he can make an appropriate allowance.

Direct methods of assessing intellectual ability — interviewing and various kinds of tests — will always be used. In interviewing it is important to give a broad coverage of the area of interests and not to form conclusions from a candidate's answers in one area only. And detachment is of course an indispensable requirement.

Job simulation tests — designed as a realistic representation of work that would be done on the job — require little explanation. One can assess performance directly. At the same time, one should bear in mind that previous experience of the sort of thing tested is important, and one should be prepared to recognise potential in those lacking such experience.

Tests of intelligence

The subject of intelligence testing is a wide one, and one that is controversial in many ways. A fuller account of what is involved is given in Appendix II. The object of this section is to explain the practical implications of test results. A designer providing tests is responsible for ensuring that a test is reliable and valid — that is that it will give the same results on different occasions and measures what it claims to measure.

The user has first to be clear what the test is measuring. Many tests measure specific skills — arithmetical ability, vocabulary and the like. Their interpretation is obvious. Others — either singly or in combination — provide a measure of general intelligence. Such a statement appears to cause a great deal of mystification. Much of this might stem from attempts to explain the notion of intelligence itself.

First of all, one should observe that any person of normal education is able to assess his acquaintances as being intelligent or otherwise to some degree. (Attempts to explain intelligence in terms of other concepts tend to be confusing and are for that reason unnecessary.) Thus an intelligent person is expected to learn quickly, to solve problems efficiently, to make a good use of his past experience in dealing with novel situations and to learn from his mistakes. An unintelligent person will not do these things. We can recognise that, between extremes, people can be placed in a rough and ready order as being intelligent to a degree.

Psychologists have no claim to be able to judge instances of intelligent behaviour in any better way than other people. The essence of their claim is that by administering tests they can arrange people in rank order both quickly and accurately. We need to bear two points in mind when interpreting results. Firstly, in everyday life we recognise the person who is intelligent but lazy or indecisive or lacking in staying power or just not very sensible. That is, we recognise the person who is intelligent but fails to achieve results because of personality defects. We can also recognise the person who is not so intelligent but gets results by doggedness, application or good judgement. A measure of intelligence is therefore only of one quality that is relevant to deciding how well a person will perform in the practical business of life. Since a test of intelligence deliberately sets out to exclude personality, we have to use our judgement to make predictions about a person's likely performance in a job.

The second point is that the effort to exclude everything but intellectual ability for testing is not always successful. A high score may be taken as valid, but people may get low ones because they misunderstood the test, were nervous and for many similar reasons. It is always difficult to establish this sort of result on firm evidence, and an assessor has to be suspicious of a candidate's claims to have suffered such misfortunes. If, however, test results are out of line with a candidate's performance, it may, in that individual case, seem right to put weight on the latter.

The essential point, however, is that a measure of intelligence is an abstract measure of ability. The quality of a person's performance in examinations, work and other situations depends on personality factors which test results ignore.

Summary

This section has emphasised the need for structuring assessments of a candidate's intellectual ability. The discussion has been in terms of a common classification — penetration, constructive thinking and judgement. Some emphasis has been given to the difficulties of assessing constructive thinking and this point is developed in Appendix I.

5.2 Working with others

5. Writing	7	6	5	4	3	2	1
6. Speaking	7	6	5	4	3	2	1
7. Working Relations	7	6	5	4	3	2	1
8. Influence	7	6	5	4	3	2	1

Communication– written and oral

A candidate's powers of communication are easily and directly assessed. Apart from the unfortunate and widespread tendency to use the ambiguous 'verbal' to mean the precise 'oral', there are no general problems.

These only arise when it seems that some correction ought to be made for a poor performance. If, for example, someone has not had practice at writing for several years, this should be borne in mind at the final assessment. One ought then to be prepared to allow for some lack of quality in expression. If the quality of thinking were there, one could foresee the quality of writing improving with practice.

Another occasional problem is that some candidates have an unfortunate idea of what is required. It has been known for a candidate to produce a stilted and bureaucratic piece in a formal test and at the same time write with spontaneity, fluency and clarity in a less formal situation. In this case an assessor would be justified in treating the latter piece of evidence as the more revealing. As far as oral communication is concerned, one has to be aware that some accents — Cockney, Birmingham, Bronx and the like — can have a negative halo effect on what is being said. An assessor has to be able to discount any immediate negative impression.

At the same time it must be acknowledged that some accents are more suited to some purposes than others. A Yorkshire accent is useful for selling Yorkshire beer. A Scots accent has a persuasive effect in selling insurance. And the authoritative quality of a BBC accent in the UK needs no emphasis.

Working relations

It is important that members of an organisation get on reasonably well with each other. Feuds and personal dislikes can be highly disruptive and must not be allowed to intrude on business.

At the same time, 'organisation men' — people who put getting on with others above all other considerations — do not make effective managers. Blandness, inoffensiveness and conformity are not the virtues to be sought. In this respect, academic research has been encouraging and has supported the findings of selectors — such stereotyped qualities are not necessary in order to achieve harmonious working relations. Such research has demonstrated that people who find themselves in each other's company tend to like each other. To this generalisation, one could of course think of obvious exceptions, one of which might be caused by a convinced disagreement on fundamental attitudes or issues — nuclear disarmers and convinced supporters of the nuclear deterrent, for example, do not naturally get on well together. While Americans are quicker to get on friendly terms, the privateness of British life is an advantage in this respect. People do not really talk about themselves on any profound level until they have already become friends and do not require others to do so.

More positively a group of people working together under some pressure — to meet a production deadline, for example or as a team of assessors — develop a liking for each other as they work for a common purpose. It is not therefore surprising that working life can make for a range of rather impersonal contacts between people who like each other well enough. This means that the minimum requirements for recruiting new members of an organisation need not be demanding. For some specialist jobs it might be put very low for people with unusual talents. In this context, people who are rather lacking in social skills can be accepted. But for some jobs, notably those in sales and public relations talents in this are an essential requirement.

On the whole, one is seeking to eliminate those with strong negative indications. Those with dominating ideological commitments are unlikely to apply for jobs in organisations which do not share their commitment. But there are candidates who are strongly self-centred and insensitive to others. There is the person who identifies efficiency with abrasiveness. Some people are sour or aggressive in their attitudes. One has to consider carefully if they will fit in.

But generally awkwardness and lack of skills are not too important given a willingness and ability to do a fair share of the work. Social skills can be acquired and a well-run organisation will set a clear example of the way things are to be said and done. These should not require unusual perception or undue effort to pick up. The essential point, however, is that blandness is not a requirement and while charm is always welcome it is not essential. The willingness to co-operate when co-operation is required and to see another point of view is vital.

So far this has dealt with people who must be rejected because of the lack of minimum social skills. But a rating scale will require the assessor to rate the candidate at a number of possible levels. He has a range of evidence to be drawn on. He may have references. (One which says that the candidate was not liked or even omits to say that he was liked is fairly rare and must be taken seriously.) Alternatively he may have an internal report and any negative comment here should be taken very seriously. He may have observed behaviour in the group or receive the opinions of other group members. These can be misleading. In particular, the short-term opinions of those under the stresses of selection are often untrustworthy.

A question often raised by conscientious assessors is how much weight they should give to their own liking for a candidate, or their dislike of him. Mature managers do not regard their immediate feelings of this sort as important when it comes to doing business with someone else. It is therefore difficult to know what weight to give them in an assessment. A first answer is that most candidates are able to make themselves pleasant when they set out to do so. Anyone who then comes across as unpleasant or unlikeable is therefore probably a difficult personality. More generally, instinctive dislikes or likes should be treated with suspicion. They are certainly not to be ignored, but the more assessors can find reasons why someone is likeable or not likeable, the more confidence they can have in their judgement.

A more difficult source of evidence to evaluate is the candidate's own account of his relations with others. Most candidates have the wit to claim that they like people and enjoy excellent relations with them. The occasional exception sometimes turns out to be striking a pose or demonstrating a private brand of humour. Clearly, such direct statements are of little value.

What the assessor has to do is to get candidates to talk about their experiences in a way which reveals their attitudes to people in indirect ways. He can, for example, ask apparently factual questions about candidates' vacation work, and obtain some indicative answers. Accounts of experiences as shop assistants, waiters and the like can be especially useful. One can ask, 'What were the public like?' and get some indicative answers. The candidate who looks mildly puzzled or irritated, and states that there were some unpleasant ones and some exceptionally pleasant ones and most were rather neutral, has probably given the most accurate reply. But one seldom gets such a reply. Some will respond enthusiastically saying how valuable and interesting the experience was. Some will give vent to a long suppressed sense of grievance or frustration, and complain at length about the lack of consideration and respect shown them and may thus reveal that they will be easily upset by the frictions of working life.

If a candidate has had experience of working in unusual conditions, accounts of these can also be highly relevant. The classics scholar from a middle class home, who has worked on a building site or in a factory will generally be able to make some useful comments about his contacts with other workers. And this also gives the assessors opportunities to explore his understanding of their attitudes and the nature of his ambitions. And, similarly, the person who has worked abroad may tell much about himself if asked, 'What is working in West Germany like?' or 'How does working in Switzerland compare with working in this country?'.

In weighing the answers to these questions the assessor is again required to interpret them with some care. He might catch a candidate in an unusual mood or occasionally trying to show what he thinks of as worldly wisdom or sophistication. He has to be on his guard against such posing and relate what he hears to the rest of what he knows about the candidate. And, of course, as in all interviews he should gently steer the candidate towards realism.

Influence

For a management job it is important to have someone who can present a case persuasively and get a point of view across to someone who may not be initially disposed to accept it. And such skills are of course particularly important in selling of any kind — goods, services, ideas or the organisation itself. This is an area where it is easy to estimate a candidate's capabilities. One knows immediately if a person is speaking or acting in a way that leads to acceptance of his arguments. One knows immediately if someone is impressing one or not.

However, there are complications in this situation. The assessor should not expect too much of a young candidate or have too demanding a model of what is required. One can think of a Churchill or Kennedy inspiring their fellow men, effortlessly persuading them that life was more exciting, that success was more likely than they thought and that their individual lives were more significant and exciting than they naturally thought. Charisma — to use the accepted term — has a value of its own, but this sort of talent is rare. Further, much management depends on the power of reasoned argument, and charisma may work by blurring distinctions and minimising obstacles.

There are those with natural gifts of persuasion and a commanding presence. But there are also persuasive skills that the person who has a basic self-confidence and a reasonable intelligence can acquire. An understanding of other people and how they react to different ways of putting things can be as important as dramatic skill. The person who is sensitive to the reactions of others and who is able to achieve their trust may be as effective as someone with more obvious talents.

The panache factor

Statistical analysis has produced a finding which most will have little difficulty in accepting. That is that some people are strong in all the traits being considered in this chapter. They are fluent in speech and on paper, easy to like and unusually persuasive. This is a valuable collection of talents — particularly useful to salesmen, politicians and public relations people — but valuable also to anyone engaged in management.

But research has further shown that assessors — even experienced and sophisticated ones — can give an exaggerated weight to these qualities in reaching their final decision. Further, not only do they do this but they often turn out to have over-estimated the degree to which the candidate possessed the other important qualities. To put the point another way, these qualities exert an unusually powerful halo effect and assessors must be aware of this.

Here the primitive belief in 'the right stuff' is at work. One can be told that the lively, entertaining and fluent candidate, who has just been seen, self-evidently has what it takes for the job. One has to repeat that high panache is no guarantee that the candidate has the other personal qualities necessary for management — drive, staying power, reliability and the capacity to grow and adapt. The belief that it is such a guarantee is a primitive superstition that no competent assessor should entertain.

This belief is not only found at the selection stage. In drawing up the specification undue weight can be put on the panache qualities. There is a popular idea of a manager as someone with physical presence, unflappable manner, always ready with the right word and always able to persuade both staff and customers that despite any appearances to the contrary all will go well in the future. Such stereotypes provide a stock character in many a television series.

The present aim is not to object to this stereotype as it stands, but to point to some of its limitations. In addition to those already mentioned, it must be pointed out that people who meet this specification must, almost by definition, be rare. It is only possible to be highly persuasive if there are a large number available to be persuaded. By the same logic an outstanding presence must be highly unusual. This gift is particularly important for bishops, generals, butlers, headteachers and headwaiters, but many of these do the job well despite an average or even poor endowment of this quality. And manifestly a number in these positions have done badly because of a lack of the other qualities required.

Equally importantly, the stereotype lends support to the assumption that a job can only be done in one way. This as already pointed out in a previous chapter ignores the plain facts of the case; that successful managers can have different approaches to the job.

More generally, there are those who perform well at interview and those who do not. There are those whose main accomplishment is performing well in interview-type situations and who have little else to offer. The reader will know of people doing a first-rate job and who thoroughly deserve promotion, but fail to get it because they cannot perform well at interview. These facts are unfortunate but they are among those that competent assessors must cope with.

Life naturally favours those who have the gift of selling themselves. Assessors need to be aware of this and give these qualities exactly the weight that meets the needs of the organisation — no less, no more.

They also have to be aware of the dangerous side to these qualities. A person who is good at persuading others may be good at persuading them that he is efficient, trustworthy and energetic when he is none of these things. One needs to be on one's guard against halo effects produced in this way.

Can panache alone be enough? In management, it clearly cannot. No one would like to claim that there are not jobs where it might be, but the writer once discussed the selection of pop groups with the manager responsible for signing them up for a large recording organisation. He said that apart from charismatic groups such as the Beatles and the Rolling Stones, there were more groups than he needed who could produce records that would sell well. Spotting such talent was no great problem. The real problem was to identify those who would perform reliably, adapt to the market and stay together long enough to produce a worthwhile return on the capital invested in them. It is salutary to remember that these are the qualities looked for in a works manager or senior civil servant.

Summary

This section has dealt with qualities that are relatively easy to assess as they are necessarily on display during assessment and working life in general. What must be emphasised in this context is the need for realism — that is, not to have an exaggerated idea of what is required, especially from the young. In this latter context one should take note of those whose opportunities for development have been limited and who can be expected to grow with experience. Assessors must be aware of the way in which it is possible to be misled by people with strong talents in this area.

5.3 Personal characteristics

9. Drive and Determination	7	6	5	4	3	2	1
10. Reliability	7	6	5	4	3	2	1

These, generally speaking, are the most difficult qualities to assess. Well-run assessment centres which seldom make serious mistakes about candidates tend to make them in this area.

The reason for the difficulty is easily explained. These are qualities that cannot be judged accurately on a short acquaintance. There is certainly a stubborn belief that this should be so. Thus, at the extreme, it is suggested that a firm handshake, a jaunty walk or a keenly returned glance to the interviewer's eye are infallible signs of a dynamic personality. In observable fact they are no such thing.

What is true is that some immediately observable qualities are loosely associated with the basic qualities required. We expect people with drive to speak in a decisive way, to hold their own firmly in argument, to take initiatives in debate and so on. But this is an area where myth is often stronger than reality. When people are asked to describe a successful manager they often describe people who play the part on television. Any established theatrical agency should be able to supply a number of people who can give a convincing performance as a dynamic manager or thrusting entrepreneur. Reliability can be suggested by a calm unflappable manner or with one conveying gritty Northern competence or with a grave manner and a reassuring Scots brogue. One meets candidates who have modelled their behaviour on such stereotypes. The simple facts are firstly, that many find it easy to simulate these qualities and so make a favourable impression and secondly, that the association is not a reliable one.

We find the notion of the secret hidden self at work here. These bits of behaviour are held to offer revealing glimpses of the hidden reality. In fact, establishing that someone is energetic, dogged or reliable enough is straightforward if he can be observed for a long enough time. What is called for, in this context, is not a keen observation of his behaviour under testing, a minute textual scrutiny of his replies to questioning or any sort of mysterious vision penetrating the secret places of the candidate's personality, but simply the opportunity to assess someone's work record for a much longer period than an assessment procedure allows.

When such observation is not possible, another sort of approach is necessary. The first step in this is to define clearly what the requirements are.

Drive and determination

This is a convenient heading for a range of qualities such as energy, stamina, application, perseverance, enterprise, initiative and the like. These are clearly important factors in a management career. The qualities looked for include the ability to work quickly and to maintain the pace when necessary for more than normal working hours. Initiative — the ability to see an opportunity or a need and deal with it — is also obviously important. Persistence — the ability to cope with setbacks or to continue with a job that is frustrating, boring, unrewarding or discouraging — is also necessary at times. For many jobs, a candidate must be able to cope not only with high pressure, but also possibly with periods of under-employment. And many people who have no problem with the former can be badly upset by the latter.

Reference has already been made to some of the ways in which mistakes are made in assessing these qualities. The 'panache factor', which has also been described, leads to others, so that, for example, people who have good oral skills and who are persuasive so that they have a noticeable social impact tend to be overrated for drive. Conversely people who are described as 'dull', 'lacking expression' or even 'lacking in life' can turn out to be highly productive and with powers of application that lead to high achievement. This is not to praise dullness or denigrate the lively and entertaining. It is simply to say that these qualities have to be assessed in their own right and not taken as firm evidence of the existence of others.

Associated with this kind of mistake is a particular model of behaviour. This is that of a person acting as he does as the result of hidden internal forces. This is implicit in some of our ways of speaking, as when we speak of someone being driven by ambition, desire or a simple bodily need such as thirst. This theory has been extended and formalised by psychologists who use it in a number of ways. However, used without an understanding of its weaknesses, it can be seriously misleading.

The assessment of drive can be seriously distorted by the implicit acceptance of some such model. On this view, a lively manner or fast speech are signs of a store of energy within. This is highly dangerous, as it is well established that a lively manner or way of talking can go with very low levels of energy and drive. In this area one should include the notion of 'nervous energy' which people sometimes use. There is no such thing. People may be dynamic or effervescent in manner, they may excite or enthral the listener, but this is no guide to the degree of energy or drive they can bring to the job. Such a manner can be seductive of the judgement even of experienced assessors, but it must be discounted in favour of the observable record of achievement.

Some evidence of the qualities required may be found in references or internal reports. The latter, especially, must be given considerable weight in this context. An assessor might override them on occasions. He might decide, for example, that a candidate has been underemployed and that faced with a challenging job he will respond more positively. But strong evidence is needed to back this sort of conclusion.

To get this sort of evidence an assessor needs to construct a careful biographical account of the candidate. What were the circumstances of his early childhood — poor, affluent or middling? Did his parents encourage him to achieve? Did they have the cash to support his endeavours? How much of his achievement has been his own? How much has been done for him? What quality of advice was available to him at the various stages of his career — 'O' levels, 'A' levels and the like? Was it assumed that he would go to a university or that he would not? Did he read a subject that seemed the natural one? Did he show enterprise and self-understanding in choosing an unusual subject? Did his family encourage his ambitions? Did they teach him to think little of himself? Did they aim to produce the perfect child? (a most destructive approach). What sort of school did he go to? What did he make of it? What opportunities have come his way and what opportunities has he created? How has he used them?

At the same time, these questions should be asked, with the necessary adaptations, of his non-work activities, travel and vacation work. When discussing a candidate's travels, for example, one can ask how he financed it — did he earn the money or did his parents pay? (or does his father get cheap air line tickets?) Did he plan everything in advance? Did he travel by train or hitch-hike? Did he encounter difficulties? Did he magnify or make light of these? And how well did he cope? An assessor can see how much initiative someone has used in getting a vacation job, whether he has gone for something safe or whether he has been adventurous.

One can see whether he has taken an interest in the firm he has worked for, how well he can rate it for efficiency and whether he has ideas on improving it in this respect.

Of course, all these questions cannot be fired at one candidate. And one is not looking for a superman who will be able to give impressive answers to every question. But one can, with developing experience and a balanced recollection of one's own youth, develop a comparative scale of achievement and so make a reasonable assessment of a candidate's performance if appointed.

Motivation

It is a common-sense requirement that anyone appointed to a job should be motivated to succeed in it. However, establishing that a person is so motivated is difficult, and is so for a number of reasons. The obvious approach is to ask, 'Why do you want this job?' or a similar question. There is no harm in asking such a question: the problems arise in interpreting the answer.

Often the answer will have been carefully prepared. And since the candidate believes that much may hang on the reply, his answer will be designed to please or impress. At one extreme the candidate may attempt high flown idealism, speaking of a dedication to the organisation and a burning desire to devote himself to its advancement. At other times the candidate may decide that realism is the thing and say that he needs a job, and from what he knows about that on offer it more or less looks as though it will suit him. Many candidates will attempt some sort of compromise between these two positions.

One might treat these answers as demonstrating the candidate's skill in answering an awkward question, but few experienced assessors would put much weight on the answers. Not only will they have been prepared beforehand to make the impression that the interviewer is thought to want, but, even if sincere, their replies will often be based on a limited understanding of what the job involves and with the younger candidate an imperfect understanding of the sort of work that will bring them satisfaction. Many organisations take pains to help candidates to learn about the job but full understanding can only come after some time on the job.

To make these points, however, is to issue a warning, not to admit defeat. The direct approach to assessing motivation is unreliable. But it could be argued with some justification that it is unnecessary. Many people who have reached high rank will freely confess that they had little idea of what the job involved when they applied, that their motivation was the need for a job and that their expressed reasons were not very relevant or even now cause them embarrassment. ('Because I want power' one now Permanent Secretary — head of a department in the British Civil Service — then told the recruiting board. He added for the writer's benefit that it had taken him half a lifetime to find out how little he would have.)

Nevertheless, it is useful to find out what a candidate is likely to give to the job and an indirect approach is then the most profitable. It is helpful to find out what understanding the candidate has of the job. A romantic or cynical view is not encouraging, but may often be dismissed as showing no more than youthful naivete.

More to the point, one may explore the areas that one covers when assessing determination and capacity for growth. Young people entering the world of work after the different world of academia have a number of adjustments to make. From being the centre of the flattering attention of lecturers and tutors they move into a situation where they are valued for their output. From a situation where they have been evaluated largely on promise, they move into one where they are appraised on their performance. And the youthful idealism which may have provided an important motive for entry to some organisations may be bruised by the realities of working life.

Most people cope with this well enough, if not without moments of strain or upset. To predict whether they will do so one must ask the same questions as one asks under other headings. One wants to know if a candidate will make a successful adjustment to the job, will acknowledge his weaker points, will not continually ascribe his failures to conditions of work or the incapacity of his bosses. One also wants to know if he will have the staying power required.

These judgements are, of course, made against the background of whether a candidate is equipped for the job. If one decides that he has the necessary qualities, that his idea of what he is coming into is reasonably realistic, that he has the necessary determination and capacity for growth, then one has covered the question of motivation much more satisfactorily than one could by direct questioning.

Reliability

It is obviously important that anyone recruited to an organisation should be reliable. That is they should produce work of the right quality at the right time and in the right quantity, despite the upsets that can occur at work and in private life. There is no great problem about this for people already working in an organisation. It is not difficult to judge if someone one has worked with for a time will be reliable or not. It might be necessary to make allowances for difficult circumstances on occasion and sometimes it will be necessary to allow for the fact that the proposed job will make greater demands than the existing one. But what needs to be done is tolerably clear.

What can be extremely difficult on occasion is to decide in the brief period of testing — five days at the outside — how far a particular candidate will turn out to be reliable. One knows well enough that most people will turn out to be reliable enough if appointed. But some individuals would not be, and an unreliable person in an important position can be very damaging. And in any position, however apparently minor, such a person can impose severe strains on colleagues and those responsible for his work. In a small group a member who cannot be relied upon can be very damaging to efficiency. However, the inescapable fact is that candidates' behaviour during testing can be unrepresentative of the way in which they will perform in the job. They may appear to be much better or worse than they would be on the job.

To set out the problem in a practical way, one might first list the main reasons why some people are unreliable. No list will be exhaustive, but the following will cover the great majority of cases:

1. Poor physical health — leading to frequent absences and reduced performance at work. This is clearly a medical matter and not a judgement for assessors.
2. Insanity — this is not always easily recognised and can be very damaging before it is.
3. Feckless temperament, general lack of conscientiousness, inability to concentrate — an endless variety of reasons are possible under this heading.
4. Inability to cope with stress — either that of the job or of private life.
5. Youth or immaturity.
6. Ideological allegiances or reasons.

7. An unusual series of misfortunes and frustrations could place an intolerable stress on the most resistant person.

There is, of course, no guarantee that a manager will not be subject to such stress and one has to recruit on the assumption that the candidate concerned will encounter no more than an average run of stresses. At the same time one must not penalise unduly anyone who has been through such an ordeal and has been shaken by it.

This is a convenient classification. The reasons for unreliability are not independent in every individual case. We have learned that much physical ill health, for example, is the result of stress, and lowered physical health may make people more vulnerable to stress. Some people by temperament are much more likely to be affected by stress than others. But this list provides a useful way of thinking about possible problems.

Difficulties arise in assessment because, as already mentioned, people's performance at the selection stage may be untypical of their behaviour in general. This may be for the following reasons:

1. They find a selection procedure uniquely stressful. They manage working life well, but the experience of being under scrutiny is for them unusually trying.
2. They are uncertain and worried about what is being looked for (despite the organisation's efforts to tell them exactly this).
3. They are over-anxious to impress, and fear that they are not succeeding.
4. The sheer unfamiliarity of their surroundings.
5. They believe that they are in an alien culture observing a set of values where their merits may be assessed in an arbitrary and unsympathetic way.

Again these are separable rather than separate factors, and a person may give less than his best for more than one reason. (In fact, the person who will put up the best performance in relation to his abilities is likely to be one who knows exactly what is required and is not too concerned about success or failure. The first factor is not related to the candidate's quality and the second is not in itself desirable.)

Enough has been said to demonstrate that accurate judgement on this point is difficult. To restore the balance one can observe that if otherwise well qualified candidates were let in without enquiry on this point there would be few mistakes. The point has been made, however, that these mistakes could have serious consequences and that some organisations recognise this by employing expert assessors for appointments where such mistakes could be very serious.

One cannot set out a complete guide to the practical problem of predicting whether a person will be reliable. This, as stated, requires the full attention of professionals. But it is possible to set out the issues involved and to warn of some of the mistakes that can be made.

Taking the reasons for unreliability in order:

Physical ill-health

This is something assessors can seldom do much about. Candidates will have signed a declaration that they are in good health. Any evidence to the contrary will have to be investigated by a doctor. Large organisations are under an obligation to employ a certain number of disabled people, but from the assessors' point of view they simply need to be identified as such.

Insanity

This is more difficult to recognise than is generally supposed. (One estimate is that the average U.S. firm takes two years to recognise this condition and do something decisive about it.) Anyone who is deeply disturbed is unlikely to get to the selection stage. Anyone who does is likely to be rejected for an unsatisfactory performance in other respects. But the extreme bizarre forms of behaviour which constitute popular ideas of insanity are unlikely to be met. It is indeed possible to work with people for some time and regard them as no more than eccentrics or nuisances rather than insane. If there is any reason to suspect that an otherwise suitable candidate is suffering from such a disability skilled investigation is necessary. On the other hand, the fact that a candidate has received psychiatric or similar treatment in the past should not be counted against him. It is possible for people to go through such phases and emerge strengthened and with a better understanding of themselves and others. Rejection is not required for efficiency; a psychiatric check is. (Anyone inclined to doubt this, might care to reflect that Abraham Lincoln suffered more than one breakdown before becoming President of the U.S.A.)

Feckless temperament

This is not necessarily apparent in a testing procedure, but is rather something to be deduced by an examination of the candidate's record. Some of the things a candidate says may appear to indicate that he is that sort of person, but some people make flippant comments under the pressure of examination and too much significance must not be given to such — one must look with care at the record. If this is one of constant changes, of unconsidered decisions, of shirked responsibilities, failures to carry a job through, then this must count heavily against a candidate.

At the same time one has to realise that there are people of feckless temperament who are good actors and quick to respond to an atmosphere. Given responsible and thoughtful assessors they are able to respond impressively in a similar way. Here again, it is vitally important not to be misled by immediate impressions at interview but to go carefully into the record. Cases such as these also run into the next category.

Inability to cope with stress

This is again a difficult quality to assess. This in part is because everyday notions of what stress is and how people react to it are rather limited. This in fact is one area where scientific advance has been substantial. (And for this reason a general account of the present understanding of the notion is given in Appendix II.)

To make a prediction in this area one has to balance a number of contradictory factors. There are no rules for doing this and it is a matter of applying skilled judgement in striking a balance for each individual case. What follows is a discussion of the more important of these factors in general terms. The first point will be readily acceptable — no more than a statement of everyday experience. This is that people vary by degree in their resistance to stress. Some are highly resistant. Some are easily upset by slight stresses. The simple division observed in everyday speech between the tough and the weak, the resilient and the brittle, is seldom to be met with. In practice, people vary in a continuous fashion.

Having made this obvious point, one must modify it with one that may be less immediately obvious. People vary in the sort of situation that they find stressful to a degree that laymen may find surprising and even on occasion comic. For some, public speaking is a pleasure; for others, an ordeal. Tough negotiators can feel helpless faced with a secretary in tears. Tough and resilient people are upset by spiders. People do not advertise such fears and our society does not encourage them to do so and a full account of what people find stressful would contain many surprises. An assessor must therefore think in terms of an order of resistance to stress among people, but also be prepared to find many individual differences in particular stresses. In the same way, making due allowances for such individual differences, one can arrange stresses in order of severity.

The following list gives stresses in roughly descending order:

death of spouse
divorce
self-destructive behaviour of family member (drugs, alcohol etc.)
marital separation
prolonged illness of family member
death of family member
personal injury or prolonged illness
loss of job
marital reconciliation

All these stresses can be much stronger if unexpected. A long awaited death is something that people can adjust to. An unexpected one will generally be a much greater shock. One should also remember that these items are not necessarily distinct. Divorce may be the result of one partner's drinking. What also needs to be remembered is that even desirable experience can bring a degree of stress. For example, marriage and promotion can bring considerable stress, desirable though these are in themselves.

This has been a list of domestic stresses. The reader will need little reminding of those in working life, but a simple classification may be helpful.

1. There is the sheer volume of work to be coped with and the need to meet deadlines. The quality must be maintained when a manager is tired, under the weather or worried by other problems. In circumstances where a person's judgement could become arbitrary a balance must be kept.

2. The job may involve conflicting responsibilities. A wider view of a problem may conflict with that which the organisation finds manageable. Appreciation of the job that ought to be done can conflict with a manager's view of what can realistically be asked of existing staff. In this sort of common situation the ability to see the different sides of a question, which is an essential requirement for

doing the job properly, becomes a source of stress and conflict.

3. Relationships with others can be a source of strength and satisfaction. They can also be a source of stress. There is no need to catalogue the ways in which people can irritate, frustrate and upset each other. What one has to bear in mind is the need to select those who will not cause an undue amount of such stress or be unduly prone to being affected by it.

4. Career pressures. Managers are normally people who are keen to achieve and to see their achievements recognised. This means that the civilities which ease relationships may conceal strong covert rivalries. And with a promotion system in which progress is very clearly marked, strong anxieties may develop in those who appear to be lagging behind. With time many will have to come to terms with the fact that they will not go as far as they expected, that the qualities they see in themselves will not be recognised and that others they may regard as their inferiors may be more successful. But the adjustment is painful and a positive outcome is not assured.

5. There are the problems which everyone supposes should be eliminated in an efficient organisation but in fact will never be totally eliminated — poor communications, lack of consultation, reversals of policy and the like.

6. Finally, there may be a conflict between work responsibilities and those of a conscientious spouse and parent. With any demanding and worthwhile job, some degree of such conflict is inevitable. With a lack of understanding on the part of the family it can become serious.

These then are some of the pressures which work in an organisation brings with it. They react with the tensions within individuals to produce the felt stresses of working life. Some people are unbothered by them. Some seem compelled to make any situation stressful.

Stressed individuals. There is a built-in tendency to see such a stressed individual as an unsatisfactory performer or as an unacceptable risk. This in part stems from a natural tendency to see 'Top People' in terms derived from descriptions of the Deity — balanced, detached and serene. As a matter of observed fact this is seriously misleading. Many people of high achievement are tense people who make high demands of themselves which, in their own view, they never quite meet. This type of person is now becoming known to laymen as 'type A', or much less accurately if more picturesquely, as 'workaholics'. Their need for achievement is never satisfied. Achievements which others find impressive, they find empty. Occasions which others find relaxing, such as a picnic, they cannot treat as anything but personal challenges. The arrangements they have made and their carrying out demand dedicated exertion. Any imperfection is a threat to their self-esteem. Many successful managers have something of this in them and many highly successful people have a great deal in them.

Candidates of this temperament do not necessarily show up well in selection. The threat of failure can produce high and obvious anxiety. The resulting impression is unattractive. The same can be true in working life. Such people can be impatient, regardless of the feelings of others in their own drive for performance and by communicating their own tensions they can make others uncomfortable. Not only is this behaviour upsetting for others, it also makes for inefficiency. Recognising the mixture of advantages and disadvantages that go with this type of personality, one is clearly faced with a considerable problem of selection. This is best done with the help of professional psychologists, but some general comments should put the problem in perspective.

Firstly, given that one is assessing an anxious person, the anxiety must be of a degree which makes for achievement. There are those whose anxiety to succeed and whose contempt for what they do achieve is of such a degree as to make them ineffectual. The essential requirement is that their anxiety should be successfully harnessed for achievement. Secondly, one must assess how far there are undesirable qualities associated with the drive to success. (These will show up in other parts of the rating scale — under 'working relations' in particular.)

One common weakness that is imperfectly recognised is the inability to cope with under-employment. Many will find it surprising that people should find this a demoralising experience, but such is the case. In some appointments such a situation might be expected from time to time, and 'type A' people are unsuitable for such situations, unless they have some outside interest which they can pursue at such times — a hobby, charitable interest, sport or the like.

Factors to be looked for at the selection stage include an ability to cover personal tensions by a genial manner or a developing awareness that other people can get useful things done without their own intense approach. Overall, as with all selection, one must not give undue weight to isolated features of the candidate's behaviour.

An overall view and balanced judgement are essential.

Young people. The problem with recruiting young people in their early twenties is that they will — most of them — have had little experience of many of life's stresses. Those they have had are likely to be connected with examinations, the study courses leading up to them and the social stresses of student life. These are not directly relevant to the job for which they are being considered. Nevertheless, someone who has coped well with them is a fair bet in regard to reliability. Anyone who has coped with some of the major stresses listed previously is a better bet. One sometimes meets a girl who has nursed a parent through a terminal illness, or a young man who has acted as a marriage guidance counsellor to estranged parents. One can have more than average confidence in their ability to cope. People who have supported others emotionally without actively seeking to be involved in emotional upheavals are also promising. On the other hand, people who have failed exams or dropped out of courses must be suspect. Stress symptoms such as continual headaches, peptic ulcer and the like must also be treated as adverse warnings.

Here the important need is to assess exactly what the stress was, and thus assess whether the reaction was a reasonable one or not. Failing exams while in the midst of a family tragedy might not point to unreliability but merely to an expected reaction. People can drop out of courses because they are lazy, silly, unreliable or because they come to a mature realisation that they were pursuing an unsuitable career path. It is much better to do this while young and adaptable than to make such a discovery late in life.

Assessing resistance to stress. In all such judgements there are two basic rules. One, do not be impressed by the candidate's manner — confident or nervous — but look at his record in detail. Two, there are no further rules. An assessor must use his judgement to the full in the light of the complete individual circumstances.

In making such a decision one must be aware of some popular theories which can mislead. Perhaps the most common might be called the 'stiff upper lip' theory. This is that the person who is cold and remote will be more resistant to stress than someone who is not. This has some truth in it. Someone who is not responsive or sympathetic to others is manifestly less likely to be upset by them. On the other hand such a cold and rigid exterior may conceal an inner turmoil of feeling.

And the theory looks at stress in one dimension only — that of the personal. It overlooks the fact that we are social creatures and in distress may gain a lot of support from our fellows. A person who can talk about his feelings and problems with ease is likely to receive help and support where a colder person will not. If one wants to think about resistance to stress in simple terms, one should add the notion of resilience to that of toughness. Someone who is in touch with his emotions, expresses them with ease and compensates for them in a mature way is the most likely to cope. In all this it must be accepted that there is often very little evidence on which to judge young people, and one is likely to have to rate them 'average' in this area for this reason.

Youth or immaturity

Our society is fairly generous in the degree to which it releases young people from responsibility. And compared with previous generations, present-day parents are both more willing and more able to insulate their children from the realities of working life. University students are accustomed to an atmosphere of mild rebellion and are not encouraged to show respect for authority. They find themselves the subject of attention from intelligent and concerned lecturers and tutors. Their fellows are more likely to admire them for their irreverence than for their sense of responsibility. Suddenly they come into the world of work, where they are valued not for the colourfulness of their personalities, but for the work they produce.

This is a severe change, and it is not surprising that some people take time to adjust to it. (Indeed it is doubtful if any of us do so fully. Most cherish the imperfectly hidden thought that their merits have not been as fully appreciated as they should have been.) Those who are the quickest to adapt or who have already adapted are not necessarily those who will give the best service in the long run. Nevertheless against this background one has to recognise the person who cannot make this adaptation and is likely to remain unduly self-centred. Such an attitude often leads to a sense of resentment, grievance or sourness which can be highly counterproductive in working life.

Summary

This section has dealt with the qualities that are most difficult to assess on short acquaintance. It has been pointed out that such judgements may tax the skills of highly trained professionals. The aim has not been to provide a quick and easy guide to becoming such a professional. Rather the aim has been to set out the relevant issues as clearly as possible. Lay assessors vary in their untutored skills in this area, but one who has digested these issues is at least equipped to avoid common mistakes.

6
Wider Considerations

The details of practical judgement having been dealt with in the last chapter, this aims to put them in a wider context. A number of issues will be considered in turn.

Sampling

A candidate is seen for a few days at the most. The assessors are attempting to predict how he will behave during many years of employment. They have to be able to decide that what they observe during this brief time is representative of a lot he will do during his career. In essence, the process of judgement involves obtaining a representative sample of his capacities. Some of the things observed are to be discarded as being non-representative and untypical. An initial awkwardness, some lack of precision in expressing a basically good idea, an inappropriate style of dress are all things that might be ignored in individual cases on the grounds that they would speedily be remedied. Such instances as these provide no great difficulties and the necessary adjustments are made without much thought.

But ensuring a valid sample is not easy and in some individual cases will require some careful thought. The activity is familiar enough. People who buy coal or corn by the 100 tons judge the quality of what they are buying from small samples. This they may do so on the guarantee of the seller that the sample is representative. Otherwise, it is obvious that careful procedures will be necessary to ensure that the proffered sample is not a misleading guide to quality. There are more homely examples. Few people buying a basket of strawberries will imagine that all the fruit is the same quality as the top layer. Gardeners know that in testing the soil of their gardens they have to be careful to get a sample that represents the garden as a whole. A sample of soil from one spot may be highly uncharacteristic. Samples from many spots are needed and must be combined carefully to get a useful result.

The same principle applies in the testing of candidates. This is most easy to see in the case of intellectual appraisals. If, for example, an assessor is seeking to assess a candidate's knowledge of current affairs, it could be seriously misleading to question him on one topic only. This may be of special interest to him or he may even have prepared it the night before. The assessor should rather question him on a number of different topics designed to cover the field. If on the other hand, the assessor is not testing knowledge but the ability to argue, he will go as deeply as possible into a couple of subjects to test the ability to deal with criticisms, see the other side of the case and so on.

For those being assessed for professional skills it is particularly important to get a wide coverage of their field of knowledge, since this after all is what they are being recruited for. Concentration on one area where they happen to be particularly strong or weak can be very seriously misleading. It may also be necessary, on occasion, for a lay member of an interviewing team to restrain the enthusiasm of a professional member who is over-keen to pursue a topic of his own to a degree which destroys the balance of the interview.

When assessing personality characteristics, the principle is the same but the application more difficult. The assessor is taking a few hours' sample from a life of something like 20 years, and making some attempt at prediction over the next 40. The way people appear to be during a selection process and particularly during an interview may be uncharacteristic. Anyone who has been through such a procedure will certainly confirm this point. The one thing that one can say with certainty after a very large number of assessments is that most people know how to make themselves agreeable when they want to do so. Otherwise appearances can be very misleading.

The most difficult characteristics to assess — drive, staying power and reliability have been discussed in some detail. The present aim is to suggest ways of getting a fair sample and, in general, this is a matter of judgement — of picking out what is significant in the individual case.

The assessor can invite the candidate to help him in this pursuit. Depending on his objective the assessor has to ask him to describe his most taxing experience, his most fulfilling one, the job he has found most interesting or the post he has found most frustrating. This however he must do with a full consciousness of what he is doing. He must be aware that the candidate will generally be trying to present himself in his most favourable light, to tell of the things which he thinks are in his favour and to avoid those which are less so. The assessor must be alert to such attempts and get a representative coverage of the ground. This is not to suggest deliberately looking for facts to the candidates' discredit. The reverse may be the case. Quite apart from the odd candidate who for various reasons may be keener on discussing his faults, one cannot rely on a candidate's judgement of what he thinks is to his credit and what is not. It must be the assessor's responsibility to get these factors in balance.

In all this it is necessary to have a sense of relevance and a sense of priorities. An assessor must be clear as to what he most needs to know. He can then devise ways of finding these out most efficiently. In most interviews time is wasted in idle chat. Whether or not a candidate can maintain an interesting conversation is of little importance, and very seldom will the time be available for so trivial an assessment.

The essential overall assessment must include a judgement, at least implicitly, that what the assessor has seen is representative of the whole. Sometimes one might reach the opposite conclusion. Someone with a first rate academic record may put up a feeble intellectual performance. Or someone reported as disagreeable and conceited comes across as pleasant and understanding. The assessor has to reconcile such contradictory pieces of evidence. And he may not succeed in every single case. Generally, however, he can make consistent sense of the whole record. The one rule, in all this, is that there are no rules. The assessor must have the confidence not to look for principles which do not exist and use his judgement to the full on the available facts.

The question of fairness

It might seem odd to have such a heading in a practical book such as this. Fairness is an ethical concept and this book does not set out to deal with ethics. Further, fairness is in part a subjective notion and the present aim is to make assessment as objective as possible. But comment is necessary precisely because fairness is subjective and different organisations may reasonably set themselves different standards. The aspect which concerns us here is the degree of attention which is to be given to the individual candidate. Every organisation needs to be aware of the costs and benefits which follow from the policy it adopts.

Whatever this may be, account must be taken of the legal requirements. In the UK these requirements can be simply outlined. With minor exceptions related to the nature of the job, discrimination on grounds of sex, marital status, nationality, race, colour, ethnic or national origin was made illegal by the Sex Discrimination Act of 1976 and the Race Relations Act of 1976. Detailed recommendations for observing these acts are made in the codes of practice issued by the Commission for Racial Equality and the Equal Opportunities Commission.

In America, the situation is much more complex, as legal requirements vary from state to state. 'Principles for the Validation and Use of Personnel Selection Procedures', published by the Society for Industrial and Organisational Psychology Inc gives a lot of useful advice together with some necessary cautions.

For some organisations there might be no problem once these legal requirements have been met. A small firm with one job on offer and a large number of applicants might reasonably decide that they could not afford to examine every application in detail, especially if there were an obviously suitable candidate.

But any organisation needs to be clear on the standards of fairness it intends to observe. Clarity of thought is necessary because the issue of fairness is not separable from that of efficiency. People's attitudes to an organisation will be affected by their understanding of its standards of fairness.

For the present purpose these are those observed in recruiting, selecting and promotion. For candidates who are asked to attend a selection procedure, both efficiency and courtesy require that they be assessed fully and carefully. Any organisation that gives the appearance of being arbitrary in its selection methods may discourage good candidates from applying. They may decide that their time will simply be wasted on a lottery. Secondly, they may decide that the rest of the firm's personnel policies work in a similar random way and their futures will not depend on their merits or the effort they put into the job. Further, any organisation which quickly writes off a candidate who has made a poor start, may be doing itself a grave disservice, for some good candidates can make a poor start for reasons that do them no discredit. For these reasons it can make good economic sense to put resources into convincing all candidates that their applications will be fully and fairly considered.

There are those who will decide that the dangers are remote or that the cost of avoiding them is too high. This is clearly their decision as far as external candidates are concerned, but for people within the organisation, such care is vitally necessary. Most people, given careful assessment, will accept the verdict of their assessors after the initial disappointment has worn off. But someone who believes that he has been unfairly treated can be very difficult to handle and may nourish a grievance for a long time. Efficiency again points in the same direction as fairness. Care must be taken to show everyone that their application has received full attention.

But not all candidates can be seen if there are a large number. It will be necessary to draw up a short list of those to be interviewed, working from the application forms and references. This is something that can be done sensibly rather than with precision and to the outsider some decisions can appear arbitrary. And to the rejected candidate they can appear prejudiced. American experience — which may be a guide to the future in the UK — has been that complaints must be expected. Apart from anything else, these complaints can be great time-wasters and careful notes of the reasons for rejecting individual candidates can be a great time-saver.

So far the argument has been in terms of fairness and its affect on attitudes. There is a more direct way in which fairness is inseparable from efficiency. This depends on the fact that many useful people are not always very forthcoming or articulate. Successful actuaries, mathematicians and computer people, for example, are often not good at being interviewed. To accept those who impress in a short interview is to accept the best salesmen. This is not the prime quality required in such people and a more persistent approach will be necessary to identify the most suitable candidates required. And, incidentally, it will be fairer to the candidates involved.

None of this has been intended to imply that any organisation should aim at the highest standards of fairness regardless of cost. Rather the aim has been to suggest that the notion of cost should not be interpreted narrowly, solely in terms of current expenditure. The way candidates are handled affects attitudes to organisations and unfavourable attitudes can cost money in many ways, even if these are not readily quantifiable.

It's common sense, isn't it?

One grows accustomed to this comment. Unfortunately the answer is not as simple as the question appears to be. But there are good reasons for agreeing with the proposition.

Firstly, anyone discussing appointment, promotion or transfer is discussing a practical management decision, and will therefore use the practical language in which we discuss such decisions. Even the psychologist, with a mastery of a wide range of theories, will reserve the language they employ for his own use. Discussing his findings he will take care to express himself in straightforward practical terms (having learned early in professional life that this is the effective thing to do.) In this respect we must therefore agree that we should be talking common sense.

The suggestion is also true in a second sense. Assessment must of necessity be an act of judgement by the assessor. There are no mechanical methods, no mathematical equations or sets of rules which will lead from observation to conclusion. The essential act is one of obtaining, ordering, weighing and balancing evidence. For this there can be no complete rules or closely specified procedure. The assessor is dependent on his own experience and judgement.

If these are the points at issue then one can hasten to agree that assessment is common sense. On the other hand, if the suggestion is that the average sensible person could do the job adequately without training, this has to be firmly rejected.

Firstly, an assessor must be as intelligent as the candidate. This is a limited and prosaic condition but it is a necessary one. Intellectually high grade candidates need intellectually high grade assessors. Much more generally, one must observe that common sense is equated with the received wisdom of the age. Anyone with a sense of history knows that much of this can date and be seen to be absurd by succeeding generations. Common sense has supported the bleeding of patients and the burning of witches. Anyone appreciating this is unlikely to be taken with the notion that our present age has achieved a unique degree of enlightenment. More to the immediate point some of the techniques used successfully by psychologists are not yet accepted as common sense and a century ago would have seemed downright nonsense. As a particular example, much of the present approach to interviewing is at odds with the approach people naturally adopt.

More directly people's common sense beliefs — on topics such as delinquency and inheritance — have been directly investigated.

The finding generally is that people hold theories of behaviour implicitly rather than being aware of them. The theories are expressed in vague and general terms so that they are largely untestable. The theories tend to be inconsistent with each other. None of these findings encourages the view that common sense is enough.

Most importantly people in general attribute the behaviour of others to their personal characteristics, while they explain their own behaviour in terms of the circumstances in which they find themselves. There is no general answer to the question of how far people react to their circumstances and how far they create them, but this is a question that must be borne in mind. An assessor must be sure that he has given full weight to the circumstances in every individual case before forming conclusions about the personality of the candidate. As already said, he should in fact look at several different situations before deciding that he has correctly assessed the candidate's personality.

Reality and existence

It sometimes happens that in the course of an assessment where abstract notions like 'intelligence', 'motivation' and the like are employed, someone will raise the discussion to a higher theoretical level by declaring that the point he is making is real. Some, for further example, declare that the reason they have given for a person's behaviour is real whereas others advanced are not. Sometimes they may argue that something does not really exist. For example, there are those at the moment who claim that motivation is not a real concept.

Such arguments are disconcerting and difficult to deal with. The simple fact is that arguments about the nature of reality and existence were well under way in Athens in 500 BC. They have continued ever since and no conclusion is yet in sight. With a practical task in hand no one wants to engage in this sort of discussion.

Fortunately, this sort of argument can easily be side-stepped. If anyone asserts that anything is real or, to the contrary, does not exist, they can be asked their grounds for making such an assertion. When they have given their reasons the discussion can be profitably pursued in terms of these reasons themselves and the use of the terms 'reality', 'existence' and the like can be avoided.

Generalisations and stereotypes

Generalisations

A lot of psychological research has been aimed at producing statistical generalisations. For example, black people are said to have lower intelligence scores than whites, and women to have higher verbal intelligences than men. This is, firstly, imprecise and misleading. What should be said is that the mean score for one group is higher than that for the other. There are many black people who get higher scores than some whites; many men with better verbal skills than most women.

It is unfortunate that statisticians are uninterested in this sort of fact and do not present figures which show them. The sort of thing that could be useful is illustrated in relation to perception of spatial relations. Here the mean score for men is higher, but it is also the case that 25% of women get a higher score than the male mean and one needs to know this if one is not to be misled. The greater problem, however, is that this information is of limited usefulness. The job is to do justice to the individual candidate. Knowing even that 99 percent of women get less than the mean male score on a particular test would not guarantee that the one woman appearing would not turn out to be one of the one percent who got more. The best use that can be made of such information is in seeing how a particular candidate fares in relation to his reference group by sex, age, race and the like. This means that it is not surprising if the result is low or high compared with candidates in general, but the usefulness of knowing this is limited.

On the other hand it is useful to remind oneself on occasion that job simulations and intelligence tests are better predictors of management performance than interview impressions. Such a reminder might help one to give the right weight to these sources of evidence when they contradict each other.

Stereotypes

The word itself is pejorative. If there is one thing we are convinced of it is that people are not stereotypes. This is absolutely right. Nevertheless, stereotypes have important uses in assessment, if, like every other device known to mankind, they are used in the right way. They remind us of the way that characteristics do occur together in a number of people.

There are, of course, bad stereotypes as well as good ones. The stereotype which consists of 'extrovert good, introvert bad', is a pernicious one, particularly as advertisements for managers sometimes require the applicant to be an extrovert. Use of the terms varies, but certainly extroverts have the pleasant and useful qualities of being warm and friendly in manner. They are generally enthusiastic in manner and colourful in speech. They are socially at ease, adaptable to changing situations and not given to worrying.

On the other hand, they tend to be impulsive and impatient. Planning and organising do not come easily to them. They tend to be slapdash and to ignore details — especially inconvenient ones. Further they are poor at analysing their own feelings and so at understanding the feelings of others. Every now and then, the wife of a man who people regard as the epitome of good fellowship breaks up the marriage announcing, to the astonishment of everyone including the husband himself, that he does not understand her. Such a woman gets little sympathy except from those who can see that once relationships call for more than immediate warmth and goodwill, such men are seriously out of their depth.

Introverts certainly have their drawbacks. They are shy, self-conscious and lacking in social confidence. They tend to be rigid in their thinking and find it difficult to adapt it and their behaviour to new situations. They worry and tend to be too concerned about the way that others react to them.

On the other hand, they have positive qualities which are necessary for good management. They find thinking congenial — both the analytic and the imaginative variety. They are patient, careful, methodical and orderly in work.

But, as the reader will have already decided, these describe extreme cases. There are few individuals who fit these descriptions closely. Most people are a mixture and successful managers need something of both in their personalities.

Many professionals, on the other hand, show strength at one end or the other of the scale. Salesmen tend to be extroverts, for reasons that will be obvious, but even here one has to be wary of stereotypes. Someone selling very expensive computers to sophisticated users will need to be more of an introvert than someone travelling in hardware or selling insurance. Research scientists tend naturally to be more introverted than most, as do accountants, actuaries and computer programmers.

Understanding such classifications is useful in two ways. Firstly, an assessor meeting someone who is warm, outgoing and confident in manner, will investigate the hypothesis that he is careless of detail. And finding someone who is careful of detail, he will want to find out if he is sociable and adaptable enough.

Secondly, knowledge of such classifications enables an assessor to understand how people can be blends of strengths and weaknesses — or more subtlely that qualities that are a strength in one situation are a weakness in others.

The problem with many stereotypes that people use is that they are accepted unconsciously and that they are not therefore tested against experience. As always, self-awareness is a necessary precondition of accurate judgement, and assessors should be explicit in making use of such devices.

Negative points

It is an unfortunate but well-established fact that a negative piece of evidence can have a wholly disproportionate effect on a selection decision. It can lead to the rejection of a candidate who might be completely suitable or even outstandingly good. Such effects are particularly marked in an interview. An unfortunate joke suggesting a flippant attitude, an attempt to be clever but suggesting a lack of integrity, or a misunderstanding showing an apparent lack of judgement can count very heavily against a candidate and, with unskilled assessors, can override any other impressions. Under the stress of an interview such mistakes are not difficult to make, and may be no more than slips of the tongue. In this context, the reason for such a lapse is of secondary importance. What is vital is to establish whether the behaviour concerned was a momentary aberration or whether it is indicative of undesirable qualities which the candidate has otherwise concealed. In an extended procedure there is time to think out ways of testing this by allocating a specific exercise to the candidate or by thinking out a line of questioning that will lead to a more balanced view of where the candidate stands.

When the issue arises in a single interview, one must be prepared to react more rapidly and adapt one's questioning to establish where the candidate really stands. If, for example, a remark suggests a harsh attitude to the handling of staff, the assessor must be prepared to ask further questions in this area, without making heavy weather of the issue and so revealing his purpose.

More importantly the candidate's record may reveal some fact to his apparent discredit — a failed exam, an apparent failure in a previous job are two of the large range of possibilities. Such facts alone can make the candidate seem an unacceptable risk. Combined with other shortcomings they can easily make rejection seem the only acceptable course. To ignore such an issue is not only inefficient selection but wholly false tact. The candidate himself may have suffered a great deal already from this apparent lapse. He may feel anxious about doing so again. He will most probably welcome the opportunity to discuss it early in the proceedings. He should be encouraged to give his view of the issue in a sympathetic atmosphere. This is not to say that his view should be accepted without interpretation. Indeed this is as vital as any part of his account of himself. But it is essential to realise that people can make mistakes and recover from them. In some cases they can learn and grow in stature as a result. The facts of the situation must be uncovered, and the candidate's development as a result must be assessed.

Opinions and attitudes

Psychologists find it useful to make a sharp distinction between opinions and attitudes. The distinction may not be immediately obvious and indeed in everyday life the division is far from exact. But the person who says 'I am not prejudiced against women, it's just that they are emotional and illogical' is stating an opinion in the first part of the sentence, and evincing an attitude in the second. Attitudes are of greater importance as they are related to the way people actually behave. People may believe that they are generous, hard-working, lazy, popular or mean and be obviously mistaken. Their own views of themselves are therefore of secondary importance.

What is more important is to find out how people are likely to behave if appointed to the job, and this involves searching out their attitudes and discounting their opinions. This is a highly skilled task for which psychologists receive careful training, and the necessary techniques cannot be described fully here.

But once the distinction is grasped it is not difficult to distinguish between the occasions when a candidate is putting forward his own view of himself and those on which he is showing how he has reacted to the situation in which he has found himself. A candidate who tells his life history as one in which he has been continually frustrated by the stupidity of others is not revealing anything about mankind in general, but may show that he is arrogant or unable to work with people. Conversely a candidate who claims to have been lucky all his life may on detailed examination show great gifts of handling people and events. In such ways people can reveal important features of their personalities.

Staff reports

This book has been written largely in terms of selection. This, it has already been remarked, is the most useful approach because it shows assessment at its most systematic and explicit. The logic of the arguments one may use can be shown with maximum clarity. For the purposes of staff reporting or job assignment the principles of assessment are the same, but the situation is rather different. Some difference of emphasis is necessary and one will review the evidence available from a different standpoint.

The first and obvious point is that one should know a person better if one has worked with him for a year than if one has observed him for two days when he is under test. Not only is the time longer, but he is seen in more natural conditions, where he is much less likely to be making a special effort or be suffering from nervousness. As a general principle it must be true that a report writer will know the person concerned better than an assessor. It is necessary, however, to be aware of some ways in which the first conclusions on a person's performance may need re-examination. Report writers will want to check the following points before reaching final conclusions.

1. The person reported on is doing a specific job with a defined range of duties. These are not designed to demonstrate the full range of his abilities in the way in which a test procedure is so designed. Neither are they designed specifically to promote his development. It may well be therefore that some of his abilities have not been displayed.

2. In particular, any judgement of capacity for growth must be based on the job that the candidate is doing. Without tests of intelligence such evidence may be limited. It has happened that a report writer has stated that a person considers his work to be below his level of intelligence and then for the test results to support this latter point of view. One therefore has to be particularly careful in assessing potential. Not only may a person be capable of better things, but also someone doing a job extremely well may not have

the necessary capacity for a higher one.

From these two points there may be any number of ramifications. Managers are expected to be versatile, but no one can be expected to be highly competent at every sort of job. For example, two people might be given a job for which they share an equal and limited competence. One might object strongly and be moved to other work. The other might carry on conscientiously achieving an uninspired performance at some cost to himself. No one would want to reward the former at the expense of the latter. Cases which show this sort of feature do occur and a reporting officer must then be prepared to make some corrections to his original appraisal.

3. It is apparently possible for some people to maintain an appearance of drive without achieving much. It is therefore particularly important to look at the output achieved rather than the appearance presented.

Most people will have adopted a particular management style because they believe that it is the most efficient and that the advantages of their style outweigh any disadvantages it might have. It may be that the particular person concerned is more affected by the disadvantages of the chosen style. Some people, for example, flourish in an informal atmosphere where they are able to use their initiative. Others like rules to work by. To report on staff in a way that will make the best use of their abilities, this kind of preference and the effect it can have on the performance of the person concerned must be borne in mind.

This last point is a special instance of the general rule that successful assessment depends on understanding oneself and where necessary correcting for one's own personal predilections.

Summary

This chapter set out to place the previous chapters in context by pointing out that any testing procedure is one for taking a sample of a person's capabilities. Even in the most thorough proceedings this will be limited. The candidate's performance during testing must be compared with all the other available sources of information in order that one may satisfy oneself that what one has observed is truly characteristic of the person concerned.

Some other general points have been discussed. The extent to which assessment might be regarded as a matter of common sense has been outlined. So has the use of generalisations and stereotypes. A warning has been given about the way in which negative points may distort appraisal and the usefulness of distinguishing between opinions and attitudes has been described.

7
Reaching the Decision

Before moving into the final discussion, assessors will have to make an assessment of the degree to which a candidate can grow. Appointed to a job some people will grow into it. Others will not. Some go downhill. Even for a specific job, as opposed to a career, it might not be possible to find somebody who is ready-made for it. In a competitive market, it may be necessary to select someone with the basic qualities necessary and train them to do the job.

Capacity for Growth

11. Capacity for Growth 7 6 5 4 3 2 1

One of the most common errors in appointing and promoting people is to fail to give proper weight to this essential factor. Such a neglect accounts for the degree of truth which we all recognise in the 'Peter Principle' — that is that people in an organisation tend to rise to their own level of incompetence. Given a number of candidates for a job, the common tendency is to appoint someone with the closest previous experience. The Principle recognises that this is an unsound approach. People performing with a high degree of competence at one level may be unable to cope at the next one up. A widely quoted case is that of the highly successful salesman, who is promoted to sales-manager and fails because of the different qualities needed. (In the best anecdotes, he reverts to salesman and works happily ever after.)

This means that a blanket judgement is to be avoided. What is necessary is an analytic approach, identifying the qualities and weaknesses which have contributed to the previous performance.

And, having made such an analysis an assessor must make a judgement of whether the candidate will grow into the new situation. This involves looking at the analysis in this light, and also looking at some further features of the candidate's personality.

By easy analogy, one can see that a candidate's performance during testing represents, at best, his capabilities at that time. What is seen will depend to a considerable degree on his previous experience and opportunities. These will vary greatly in relevance from candidate to candidate and may afford a poor guide to the performance to be seen over a lifetime's career. Any procedure which does not consider a candidate's capacity for growth is implicitly assuming the contrary.

This, therefore, is a vital judgement. It is obviously vital from the point of view of fairness involving the recognition that not everyone has had an equal opportunity to show what they are worth. Perhaps less obviously, it is also necessary for efficiency. If assessors assume that what they see is straightforwardly representative of the candidate's performance on the job, they are letting themselves in for some disappointments and are likely to reject some highly talented people.

At this point it is worth reflecting on the job to be done. One can be looking at people in their early twenties and younger. Many will still have some labile adolescent attitudes. (A significant proportion describe themselves as 'cynical' — this generally means no more than they have yet to get to grips with practical life.) They will have few years of self-aware life behind them. They may be being assessed for a career of 40 years. Looking at assessment in this way one can readily see that present performance is not necessarily the best guide to the next 40 years.

This is obviously the case when one considers that people of equal ability may have had a very different start in life. At one extreme, there is the child of prosperous and cultivated parents with a first rate school and university education, with a full range of stimulating social contacts and wide opportunities for travel and cultural growth. At the other end of the scale there is someone from a limited home background, where, for example, any sort of intellectual pursuit is strongly discouraged, and with a very limited education. The former should perform at a much higher level, and direct comparison with the latter would be misleading. Assessors must estimate how well each would be doing after a time in the organisation. They should look for competence within a fairly limited period and might see much greater achievement after a longer time.

A geometric model might make things clearer. For simplicity's sake both candidates are shown as at the same level of achievement. One has done what might be expected. The other has clearly achieved a great deal more and can be expected to go yet further in the following years.

Figure 7.1:

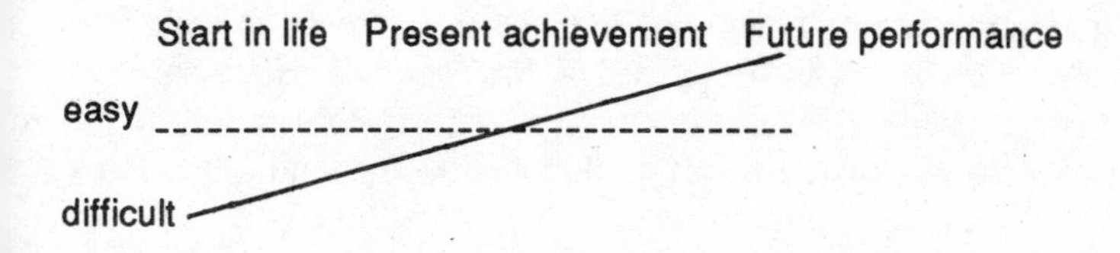

This, of course, is far too simple a picture. There are many other factors to take into account, not least of which is the fact that many people with an easy start in life respond and grow when the pressure is on and they experience responsibility. But the model does illustrate the nature of the job in some important respects. What one is engaged in is a purely technical exercise, attempting to project a person's development into the future. When this has been done one has done exactly as much as fairness requires.

Assessors are not engaged in a moral exercise. Emphatically they are not awarding consolation prizes to those whom life has treated harshly. They must be careful to remain unmoved by such misfortunes however severe and however bravely and constructively they have been met. They must find basic abilities, the means of improving them and a willingness to improve.

As a matter of practical fact, it is generally easier to recognise the person who is unlikely to grow. Indicative points are a grossly inflated idea of his abilities, or self-criticism carried to a self-destructive degree. A defensive or aggressive attitude to the criticism of others is also a bad sign. There is also the person who simply seems to have reached his limit with a comfortable and complacent view of his achievement, someone who appears to have reached middle-aged attitudes towards his own development very early in life. In short, this is someone who has decided that he does not need to grow and will not therefore do so. As already said, this is among the most difficult judgements to be made. Knowing how people can grow or fade, one is bound to be dissatisfied with what one is able to do. Nevertheless, there are many questions that should be asked and a significant amount that can be done to answer them.

To judge how far a person can grow into what the organisation needs, one looks for:

1. On the intellectual side, someone receptive to new ideas — about himself, about society and the situation in which he works. As far as pure intellectual potential is concerned, the best estimate is given by a test of general intelligence. The amount of weight to be put on such a measure depends on the degree to which one sees the job concerned changing during the candidate's career. If the changes seem likely to be small, then one would tend to put more weight on his present performance. If it were thought that the job would change in ways that could not be clearly foreseen then this measure — as an estimate of intellectual versatility — would be highly relevant.

2. A willingness to exploit opportunities and accept new responsibilities.

3. A willingness to take a long view and to delay rewards until something has been achieved.

4. The right balance of fundamental self-confidence and moral conviction so that a candidate can

   a. modify his beliefs and standards without compromising his basic integrity.

   b. change directions when necessary and not persist with aims that then become irrelevant. In particular, he should not be the sort of perfectionist who cannot abandon a scheme which has become uneconomic.

   c. co-operate in new groups, committees, roles and situations meeting their needs, but retaining enough of himself to continue to make a contribution as an individual — not to become a trimmer or yes-man.

   d. Work with others without letting the inevitable compromises obscure the longer view.

5. A willingness and an ability to communicate with others including, in particular, the much less bright or the less willing.

Like all such lists this describes an impossible person. All these qualities will seldom be found in one individual. What one looks for is the degree and balance among them that will make growth possible. More to the immediate point it will often be difficult to discern and weigh these qualities in the hopeful 21-year-old. There will be cases where a clear judgement can be made. More generally with such people, one can check the absence of negative indications and assume a fair capacity for growth.

With some complex young people this judgement is particularly difficult. Assessors can meet candidates at such an age who have yet to resolve a number of conflicting tendencies within themselves. For anyone committed to the view that one needs single-minded people for the job, this will be a strongly negative point. On the other hand, anyone who takes the view that society and the world we live in are complex and that we need people with a range of understanding — a need to understand views which may be those of a minority, unpopular or poorly understood in general — will be prepared to give greater consideration to such a candidate. One assessor put the point graphically in recommending one such candidate: 'The best orchestras sometimes take the longest to work in harmony.' Those with the greatest potential for understanding their fellow men may take longer to co-ordinate their own attitudes. These may be the best people to work abroad in a society that needs a lot of understanding or best able to appreciate the needs of foreign customers. They may have the right kind of imagination to work with racial minorities in this country. There are other kinds of difficult cases, where people have strong qualities but have serious weaknesses which mean that they are not ready-made to go far in the job. The 'type A' personality has already been mentioned, where dedication to the job can be in conflict with an inability to understand other people sufficiently well. Here a longer view of the candidate's usefulness may have to be taken.

This is not to advocate the recruitment of neurotics and those in perpetual conflict with themselves. Rather it is to suggest that it can sometimes be valuable to take a longer view of a candidate of ability who might otherwise seem inadequate in this respect. Movement in the direction of maturity must be visible and a benign outcome predictable. But precocious maturity is not always desirable.

With older people the question of possible growth is a vital one. The simple fact is that people do become less adaptable and flexible as they grow older. But it is equally a fact that they vary widely in this respect. Some become set in their ways very quickly. Others retain a flexibility of mind until retirement. It is therefore particularly important to assess an older person's capacity for growth. For job assignment and promotion, there is a great deal more evidence on which to make this vital assessment.

The decision

The final decision may come after an extended interview procedure, after weeks or even months of careful thinking, or it may come after an interview board lasting no more than half an hour. This means that the time that can be taken over a final decision may be anything down to something like five or ten minutes. In this last sort of case clearly the steps of the appraisal must be more arbitrary, but it does mean that skill and judgement are required to make the best use of the time — to decide what must be discussed and what must be taken for granted.

The objective of this section is to outline the procedures required for a sound decision that makes full use of the available evidence. The assessors must decide, in each individual case, what must be omitted because of the constraints of time. This constraint, it should be made clear, is the only allowable reason for omitting any of the procedure.

Legend of course has it otherwise. Having achieved effortless and immediate insights — so it goes — the assessor goes on to produce confident and infallible judgements. In real life this is the reverse of the truth. Assessors are faced with a session of work that may be intense and demanding. This involves the careful assembly and weighing of a mass of evidence.

Unfortunately, legend is reinforced by a number of other factors. Firstly, sheer ignorance can play its part. So much selection is done by people with no aptitude or preparation for the job. This lack of preparation is often combined with the belief that somewhere, somehow there are assessors who are quick and infallible and one should attempt to model oneself on them.

More immediately even good assessors are under pressure at this point and may react by simplifying the problem without being aware that they are doing so. This, it goes without saying, is a tendency to be resisted.

Recapitulation

As part of the process of assessment the assessor will have read the application form, references and reports with care. He will have formed hypotheses for investigation and tested these carefully as part of the process. He will have formed judgements on the candidate's individual qualities taking care not to confuse them with other desirable qualities; but assessing each quality in its own right. Any negative impressions received during the process will have been investigated with special care and either confirmed or discarded. The performance of the candidate in all parts of the procedure will have been assessed at its face value. And at the same time the assessor will have noted any reasons for thinking that this represented something better or worse than he was likely to get in the longer run — whether what he saw was, in fact, a good sample of the candidate's behaviour.

This involves a mass of details to be worked through and digested. Various devices are available for this purpose — score sheets, standardised biographical records, systematic interview reports and the like. These all have their uses depending on the procedure followed.

The one device that cannot be sensibly dispensed with is a rating scale. This ensures that the most relevant qualities have been considered, provides a sensible structure to what otherwise can become an untidy and repetitious debate and provides a simple and efficient way of summarising and comparing the merits of different candidates.

At this point the assessors begin their final conference. There is a natural order for this. First, the candidate's previous record should be reviewed. In what circumstances did the candidate begin life? What has he achieved? Is there evidence that his achievements are his own or the converse? Were any notable opportunities missed or created? Next assessors should check that their records of his performance — scores obtained in intelligence, job-simulation or other tests are in agreement.

From this they should work through the rating scale item by item, taking it in turns to declare their ratings. A difference of one grade is not significant, but where larger differences are found, the evidence should be discussed with the objective of reaching agreement. On occasion, however, where the candidate's performance is complex, a spread of ratings might give a better picture. One candidate, for example, was found to write clearly and interestingly when he had time to re-draft his first thoughts. When under pressure so that he did not have time for such re-drafting, his written work was poor. The assessors decided to represent this difference by a spread of marks from 'above average' to 'below average'. In cases where a candidate has shown energy and enterprise but a lack of staying-power a similar spread for 'Drive and Determination' would represent this finding.

Working through the scale assessors should remember to use all the evidence available — combining that from the candidate's past record with that from his performance during assessment. Generally these sources will be more or less in accord, but there will be cases where a conflict has to be resolved. Where a candidate has done well in the job-simulation tests, but has a poor academic record, the assessors might be in a position to agree that he was not fully engaged in academic work. Conceivably they might have reasons for taking an opposing view. They might decide that he comes alive for a short stimulating test, but shows no staying power when the task is longer.

At the same time, assessors have to remember to relate the qualities to the job involved. A research scientist, for example, requires a different sort of judgement from that of a general manager or a salesman. 'Constructive thinking' will cover different ground for an engineer and someone in advertising.

With the Rating Scale complete, the process moves naturally into the last stage.

At this point the assessors weigh the candidate's qualities against the job or career requirements. Does he fit them or does he not? The answer to this might be under two headings. Is he capable of doing the immediate job? How far and fast will he grow if appointed?

Figure 7.2: A clear pass

1. Penetration	7	6	(5)	4	3	2	1
2. Constructive Thinking	7	6	(5)	4	3	2	1
3. Judgement	7	(6)	5	4	3	2	1
4. Numeracy	7	6	(5)	4	3	2	1
5. Writing	7	6	(5)	4	3	2	1
6. Speaking	7	6	(5)	4	3	2	1
7. Working Relations	7	6	(5)	4	3	2	1
8. Influence	7	6	(5)	4	3	2	1
9. Drive and Determination	7	(6)	5	4	3	2	1
10. Reliability	7	6	(5)	4	3	2	1
11. Capacity for Growth	7	6	(5)	4	3	2	1

Sometimes the answer will be immediately clear. If one job is available and one candidate is outstanding, then the decision will be obvious. Where selection is to a standard, for an entry grade for example, more careful consideration might be necessary. But some candidates will not require much thought.

This shows clearly an outstanding candidate who will certainly be acceptable. (Unless there is some very good reason not shown in the profile — poor health or evidence of lack of integrity, for example. Such cases are rare.)

Conversely there will be a larger number of obvious failures as a larger number of candidates will be well below average and clearly unacceptable. (The logic of this depends on the fact that, as a rule of thumb, most organisations will invite about five candidates for each vacancy. This in practice means that a candidate who is clearly above average will normally be acceptable and anyone clearly below average will certainly not be.)

The person specification

In between these extremes there will be candidates who require more thought. Here a careful comparison of the person with the person specification is necessary. (In theory, the person specification should encompass the job description. In practice, it can be more convenient on occasion to use the latter.)

At this point the emphasis must be on realism. There are very few wholly convincing candidates. With even the best there is often an area or two of doubt, and it is not difficult to come up with reasons — good, soundly based reasons — for rejecting them. It is at this point that a job description can be something of a hindrance to efficient selection. It can always be used to find a candidate wanting in some important respect. What one can do more profitably is think in terms of the people who are actually doing the sort of job under consideration — making, of course, the necessary allowances for age and growth. Sometimes an assessor can call to mind a colleague who shows much the same pattern of strengths and weaknesses as the candidate and who manifestly is performing competently.

Anyone who talks glibly of raising standards and attempts to do so by making them impossibly high must be firmly discouraged and led back to realism. Sometimes an assessor will agree that the profile looks good but then declare that the candidate is unacceptable because he lacks some essential quality such as 'flair' or 'sparkle'.The assessor has then to be reminded that while he might be talking about a desirable quality this is beyond what the agreed specification calls for. At such times, the specification, which otherwise can often appear to be a rather obvious and uninteresting work of piety, really earns its keep.

In parallel with this one must remember that a job can be done in different ways. Some will achieve by application and study what others will achieve effortlessly by flair. Some may manage staff by example and inspiration, others will achieve the same results by careful instruction and a sympathetic understanding of problems. Some will work fast in short bursts, others will be dogged and painstaking. Assessors should forget popular stereotypes. They should forget about the TV characterisations of thrusting managers and the like and think of the people who actually succeed in the job. What matters is the job done, not the method of doing it.

The whole person

So far the emphasis has been on the careful accumulation of evidence and the care needed to avoid confusing one characteristic with another. At the final stage, the emphasis changes. Assessors need to see the candidate as a whole. At this stage it becomes clear that the candidate is more than the sum of his individual qualities. One cannot reach a decision by any mathematical process of weighting individual judgements. As one sees the whole picture the significance of the parts may change and individual pieces of information may change an existing picture in a dramatic way.

These are abstract points. Some concrete examples should clarify them. Take for instance, a candidate with high gradings for penetration, personal contacts, influence and drive. This points to a very promising candidate. Now add the observation that this is a person of poor judgement. This changes the overall picture drastically. Instead of a promising candidate one has a menace. The attractive qualities of drive and persuasiveness become sinister qualities when applied to selling and implementing unsound ideas.

This sort of effect means that simple mechanical models of the way in which the evidence is finally assembled and weighed — putting together the jigsaw or filling in the crossword — are inadequate. They are acceptable in so far as they emphasise the need for care and patience. They are seriously misleading when

Figure 7.3: A menace

1. Penetration	7	6	⑤	4	3	2	1
2. Constructive Thinking	7	6	⑤	4	3	2	1
3. Judgement	7	6	5	4	3	②	1
4. Numeracy	7	6	⑤	4	3	2	1
5. Writing	7	6	⑤	4	3	2	1
6. Speaking	7	⑥	5	4	3	2	1
7. Working Relations	7	⑥	5	4	3	2	1
8. Influence	7	6	⑤	4	3	2	1
9. Drive and Determination	7	6	⑤	4	3	2	1

applied to the final view of the candidate, and anyone subscribing to them will be fatally restricted in his thinking.

For a further example, a candidate had recorded that her father was an engineer and that the family owned a yacht. These with other details suggested a comfortable background, which made her competent academic progress through a select Oxbridge college seem unexceptional. Her performance on assessment was borderline. The picture at this stage was of a person who had had every chance in life and was performing at a rather uninspired ceiling. In the last of her interviews, it came out that her father was the sort of engineer who did minor electrical repairs. The yacht was a rather modest vessel, which had been largely financed by her vacation jobs and she had skippered it with considerable dash and enterprise. As further details were added, the total picture changed to one of a young woman of achievement, who might have considerable potential for growth.

A less dramatic and more typical case was that of a candidate who appeared pugnacious and dogmatic in a simulated committee. In interviews it emerged that he came from a dockers' community, and that the rest of the family were dockers. He had had no experience of any kind of committee work and his inappropriate behaviour in the committee test was unsurprising. When, face to face, he turned out to be responsive and thoughtful, it became clear that an alternative view of his future growth was possible. Depending on which piece of evidence one took as significant, one had an overall picture either of someone incapable of fitting into working life or someone rather more promising.

The way in which one holds the essential facts in mind and forms alternative overall views is not necessarily conscious. It is common enough to go to sleep with a mass of facts in mind and wake up with a clear view of the candidate. The only point to be made here is a negative one. Assessors should not be tied by any prescriptive view of what thinking is like but follow any method that suits them (a point given fuller treatment in Appendix I).

But having formed a view of the candidate, an assessor must treat this as a hypothesis to be tested. In some cases, as already suggested, there may be alternative views to be tested. The essential point here is that, however intuitively these views have been reached, they must be checked carefully against the observed facts.

In reaching a decision the assessor has to use his range of committee skills to the full. Disagreement must not be shirked on any significant issue. The argument should not be prolonged on lesser considerations.

Sometimes at the point of decision it turns out that a vital piece of information is missing, that the evidence available is mixed or ambiguous in its interpretation. In an extended procedure this risk is minimised by conferences between assessors so that such doubts can be identified in time and resolved. Any procedure, however brief, should be carefully planned towards this end. Nevertheless, such problems do arise and assessors must be prepared to deal with them. Not to be encouraged are intuitions that the candidate will 'be all right' or has 'got what it takes'. People who rely on these have a marked tendency to forget the occasions when they go wrong. Such intuitions may work on occasion — sometimes as a matter of luck and sometimes because they are based unconsciously on a valid stereotype — but they are not to be relied upon. This is clearly something that is better done consciously with an explicit weighing of the chances and penalties of being wrong. Sometimes assessors can decide that if they are wrong the consequences will not be disastrous.

For example, assessors might be worried that a candidate will not adapt to the organisation. If this is a person who is not very enterprising, the risk of appointing someone who is likely to hang on as an inefficient member of the organisation is clearly a high one. On the other hand, a lively and enterprising person could probably be relied on to move elsewhere if dissatisfied and so this risk would be a lesser one.

If there is a general rule, it must be that if a risk is to be taken, it should be taken on a candidate of otherwise high quality. With professionals quality in the professional field would be the obvious factor that might justify taking risks over a more doubtful area. For barristers, salesmen and public relations people, panache might be held to outweigh potential weaknesses in other areas.

This quality, it has been argued, is a more doubtful one to take a risk on when selecting a manager. The qualities which are important will vary with individual organisations. The British Civil Service traditionally placed intellectual quality above others — which preference some see as the source of some of the country's present problems — but this tendency has been much less marked in recent years. Notoriously, there was a time when some American firms put the main emphasis on working relations — a tendency that is notably weaker since it was exposed in *The Organisation Man*.

For most organisations, the most useful quality is probably a record of coping — with difficulties, ambiguous situations — and exploiting opportunities. Napoleon declared that he wished to be served by lucky generals. He was, of course, making sardonic reference to the excuses made by the failures. Someone with a record of success, of coping with problems or of turning set-backs to his advantage, has a lot to balance against possible weaknesses.

At the same time, it is vital to distinguish between weaknesses that might be corrected by training or experience and those that cannot. A very good accountant, who is not very fluent at explaining technical points, might be taught how to do so. An arts graduate who is not practised at handling numerical information might easily learn how it is done.

And some faults might be acceptable in some jobs. It is not easy or always possible to teach a self-absorbed person to get on with others, but weakness of this kind would probably be acceptable in an able laboratory researcher. And a first-rate salesman who has his own ideas on working hours might be a profitable investment.

Sometimes the problem will be obvious from the profile.

This shows a potentially good bet, spoilt by poor working relations. Much depends on the reasons for this rating and everything else depends on the balance between this weakness and the candidate's good qualities. If the candidate is self-centred and aggressive, then rejection seems likely. If he is a shy person from a restricted background, who can be expected to thaw out then there is a better case for acceptance. But the final verdict has to depend on the details of the case.

Sadly assessors are not paid to take interesting risks. One would not be alone in regretting this. But there must be solid evidence of the basic qualities required. If a candidate does not have these, then

Figure 7.4:

1. Penetration	7	6	(5)	4	3	2	1
2. Constructive Thinking	7	6	(5)	4	3	2	1
3. Judgement	7	6	(5)	4	3	2	1
4. Numeracy	7	(6)	5	4	3	2	1
5. Writing	7	6	(5)	4	3	2	1
6. Speaking	7	6	(5)	4	3	2	1
7. Working Relations	7	6	5	4	(3)	2	1
8. Influence	7	6	5	(4)	3	2	1
9. Drive and Determination	7	6	(5)	4	3	2	1
10. Reliability	7	6	(5)	4	3	2	1
11. Capacity for Growth	7	6	(5)	4	3	2	1

rejection is required. Assessors can make allowances for many things. The talent can be rough and ready, the self-presentation poor, the skills of communication underdeveloped, but the total picture must be one of someone who can put up a sound and reliable performance upon appointment.

The final mark

If the candidates are being assessed for just one job, then they can be arranged in an order of merit. But where any number of candidates is seen, some way of putting them in an order of merit is useful. An alphabetical scale is preferable as, unlike a numerical one, it heads off any tendency to arrive at it by any sort of averaging or other mathematical technique. Where a few candidates only are involved a simple A,B,C might be enough. For a procedure that involves several groups something longer is desirable. The following scale has much to recommend it.

A - well above acceptable
B - more than acceptable
C - acceptable
D - near-miss
E - below acceptable
F - well below acceptable
G - hopeless

Here A and G will seldom be used but they make the use of the other five more likely. The near-miss mark 'D' is useful because it provides a reserve list of people whose papers might be re-examined for appointment if there is a short-fall of acceptable candidates. When the system is organised so that the assessors make recommendations to higher management who take the final decision, these are the candidates who would naturally be considered for upgrading.

Summary

In making the final judgement assessors must again ignore all the legends that suggest that this is a simple and instinctive process. They are involved in a careful comparison of the candidate and the job requirements. They need to resist any pressure to make the process brief or arbitrary. Two requirements must be borne in mind. The first is the need for realism, to avoid using person specifications in too rigid a way, to have a down to earth knowledge of the qualities that make for success on the job and appreciate that any one job can be done in different ways. The second is the need to see the candidate as a whole, to avoid applying any sort of averaging or adding process to ratings of the candidate's qualities.

As part of the overall judgement an assessor has to decide how far the performance he has seen is characteristic of the candidate and if it has in any way been affected by the special features of the selection procedure. Equally importantly, he must make a judgement of the degree to which a candidate can grow.

He must also be ready to handle cases where after considering every possible factor he is in a state of genuine perplexity. Such cases may not be common but they are important.

8
The Summing Up

For those with an interest in their fellow men and women, assessment is a fascinating and rewarding activity. There are great satisfactions in selecting the right person for the right job, in achieving an understanding of a puzzling candidate and in finding useful potential in an individual where it was previously unrecognised. There can be moments of excitement and discovery, but the process is not the glamorous and effortless one of popular legend and imaginative fiction. In contrast to such accounts, this book has argued that assessment must be systematic, careful and self-questioning. Hard work is necessary and unavoidable.

On the other hand, it has attempted a constructive approach, suggesting that the activity is a rational one, where care and hard work are repaid and where assessors can continuously improve the quality of their assessments.

One point has not been given any prominence and this is our sheer ignorance — both individually and collectively — of the ways in which other people may behave and how they may adapt and grow. This has not been a deliberate avoidance but rather an assumption that the point is too obvious to need emphasis. In any useful guide such emphasis must be on what can be done — the difficulties are obvious enough. There is, however, a practical point to be made. We must on occasion accept that a decision is unsatisfying — if we knew more about the candidate or understood what we had observed we could have taken a better founded decision. There are occasions — especially when we reflect that the decision will have important consequences in someone's life — when this sense of inadequacy may weigh heavily upon us.

We have to accept that we are in the same position as we might be when faced with many other management problems — that of taking a rational decision based on insufficient evidence. We are bound to make mistakes and, further, we can make these errors when we are confident of our decisions.

Assessors could take comfort from this. If we could look at the raw young man or woman of 20 and predict exactly how they would fare over the next forty years, life would be a rather sad affair. As it is, we can take comfort from the way people grow and exceed our expectations. And, if they under-perform in relation to such expectations, this makes the same essential point. People are complex beings. They are flexible and adaptable. Their performance varies, and they can often be puzzling.

This means that one must suffer one's defeats. No one is exempt from failure on this undertaking. The best assessors are well short of infallible; they simply make fewer mistakes than others. But one can learn from one's mistakes. Indeed, one also learns from one's successes. This is the essential intellectual fascination and reward of assessment. One never stops learning.

Appendices

I Thinking

Analytic and creative thinking

'Thinking' covers a range of activities. The two that are important for the present purposes and need to be distinguished are analytic and creative thinking. In these terms, the distinction is obvious, but unfortunately when people think about thinking, notions applicable to the first sort — analytic thinking — are applied to the second, and this leads not only to serious confusion but also limits their ability to think in a creative way.

Analytic thinking is rational, precise and clear. Creative thinking is none of these. It is confused, unclear and can often be startlingly irrational, silly or facetious at first sight. This point is clearly illustrated by the well known story of Kekule and the benzene ring. Benzene had puzzled chemists for many years. At the time they knew only about organic compounds which had a straight chain structure such as the paraffins.

$$
\begin{array}{ccccccc}
 & & H & & H & & H & & \\
 & & | & & | & & | & & \\
H & — & C & — & C & — & C & — & H \\
 & & | & & | & & | & & \\
 & & H & & H & & H & &
\end{array}
$$

To form a stable relationship such as this there had to be more than twice as many hydrogen atoms as carbon. As the numbers approached equality the compounds became increasingly unstable. Benzene had been shown to contain 6 atoms of carbon and 6 of hydrogen and it should therefore have been explosive. But it was relatively stable.

Kekule became deeply involved with this problem (which had been known to chemists for many years) but the answer eluded him. One night he ate a lobster supper and travelling home on a bus began to feel ill. He saw pink snakes. Suddenly they bit their tails and it came to him in a flash that the carbon atoms were arranged in a ring. Subsequent testing proved the point and explained the relative stability of the compound.

What thinking is really like

This story is often told as a joke against Kekule or in an apologetic way as an example of an aberration of scientific thought. However, it is only a rather extreme case of normal thinking, and it happens to offer a neater anecdote than most. For this reason, the fact that an idea is prima facie facetious or silly is not enough to rule it out as a potentially useful one. The puzzling thing is that, while people know very well that their own thinking is like this, they should suppose that other people's can be effortlessly creative and obviously right. We all know that original ideas seldom come to us in a ready-made and acceptable form. Very often one can see both that an idea is going to be helpful and that, as expressed, it is unlikely to be accepted. Often one has to put in a lot of work before an idea is in the right form to appear before a critical audience.

Producing arguments for those who do not accept this is difficult. The difficulty is the familiar one that one has when somebody denies what appears to be an obvious part of everyday experience. What follows will read like a statement of the obvious to some, but it may show some understanding of the objections.

One might quote authority in support of this view. Waismann (1), for example, once claimed that no original thought had been expressed precisely. Koestler summarised his view of scientific discovery in the title of his history *The Sleep Walkers*.

But it is probably more fruitful to discuss the reasons that lead people to think that, in an ideal sense at least — if not in their own experience — creative thinking is a smooth and rational process.

Firstly, there is the model of logic. This follows strict rules, one can do it as one does mathematics and once one has grasped some simple rules it is fairly easy. But we should note that the language we use to describe the way we think is much wider than the terms of logic. We certainly may mention premises and describe deductions as do logicians. But we talk also of groping for ideas, of refining a crude thought, of trying to clear our minds, hitting on a solution and trying an idea out. And all these lack the precision of the logician's terms. True, we often submit the results of our thinking to logical rules, but this is a critical activity, and logic does not help with producing original thoughts.

To say that a piece of thinking is logical is indeed to praise it.

But to assume that all praiseworthy thinking is logical is to commit an elementary mistake of logic.

Secondly, people generally have the wit to work on their original crude ideas until they are socially acceptable. Goffman writes '...where the individual presents a product to others, he will tend to show them only the end product, and they will be led into judging him on the basis of something that has been finished, polished and packaged ... it will be the long tedious hours of lonely labour that will be hidden'. (2) Certainly on occasion one can marvel at the aptness of a retort, but original wits produce bad jokes as well as good. And history is selective. No one has preserved Oscar Wilde's conversation when he was suffering from a hangover, or recorded Bernard Shaw's talk on a wet Wednesday afternoon.

Original thinking then is untidy, and is not to be achieved by following rules. People have to unlearn much that they were taught at school and develop their own methods. But having got what they set out to get, there remains the difficult job of persuading others to accept the new idea. Physicists, mathematicians and the like are fortunate in this respect because their notions can be tested by reference to accepted rules.

In practical affairs, evaluating and accepting new ideas are difficult processes. This is simply because new ideas appear as contrary to common sense — they offend the practical judgement which people have to develop. This must be true by definition since common sense represents the collective wisdom up to that time.

One manager who had his successes wrote '...there is nothing more difficult to carry out, nor more doubtful of success, nor more dangerous to handle, than to initiate a new order of things. For the reformer has enemies in all those who profit from the old order, and only lukewarm defenders in all those who would profit by the new order, this lukewarmness arising partly from fear of their adversaries ... and partly from the incredulity of mankind who do not truly believe in anything new until they have had actual experience of it.' (3)

Certainly, introducing a new idea calls for skill and resource. Generally, one tries to show that it is really only a variant of received truth, or that one's hearer knew it all the time or thought of it himself. These approaches are generally more efficient than assuring the customer that new techniques will bring him great advantages, as this last point can seldom be demonstrated, but this in its turn leads to problems.

The criterion of success is that the novel idea be accepted as common sense, as something simple and obvious. This means that it then becomes difficult to demonstrate that anything new has been produced. This is easily observed in teaching science.

Often the most difficult task is to describe the state of the science before the discovery concerned. Organic chemistry before Kekule and psychology before Freud are very much cases in point. The critics of the latter, in particular, are seldom aware that when they attack him they do so in terms which did not exist before he introduced them. This is probably even more true in management, where the most efficient techniques often involve concealing the novelty of ideas. And the better the idea the more obvious it might appear.

The best model we have for thinking in this context is not that of a logician making machine-like deductions or of (say) the Wright brothers producing their aeroplane to instant acclaim. Rather one should think of Sherlock Holmes spending long hours of pondering before springing to his feet and cursing himself for having failed to spot the obvious.

All this being so, it should be no surprise that the assessment of a candidate's ability to produce new ideas should be so rough and ready. To produce a novel idea in an acceptable form takes a long time in relation to the time-scale of an assessment procedure. Most candidates themselves, aware that most of the ideas they can produce are unfinished and that they are being tested for judgement, will be prudent enough to keep silent. And one must accept that this is the prudent course. Therefore, anyone wishing to assess this quality thoroughly must do so in a context where the candidate is not being simultaneously assessed for judgement, and knows that he is not being so assessed.

This is clearly a very difficult situation to set up. In any short procedure it will be impossible, and one has to rely on other sources of information.

References

1. F. Waismann — Then Oxford University Reader in the Philosophy of Science, formerly of the 'Vienna Circle'.

2. E. Goffman — 'The Presentation of Self in Everyday Life', Pelican 1957, p. 53.

3. The Secretary to the Second Chancery of Florence, 1498-1511 — N. Machiavelli in 'The Prince'.

II Intelligence

A lot of trouble has been caused by people attempting to answer this question with a brief dictionary-like definition. In a general sort of way, people know what intelligence is already, and such brief definitions which concentrate on one aspect only tend to confuse the reader. The sort of question that people want answered is how intelligence can be measured. How can anyone put a figure on anything so abstract and nebulous? And if we can derive such a measure what can we do with it? These are the questions that will be answered.

Normal use of the term

a. People describe some performances and some people as 'intelligent'. There is a large amount of agreement about such verdicts. Intelligent people learn fast, use their past experience effectively to deal with new situations, avoid repeating mistakes, do well in examinations and so on. As with any such judgement we are striking some sort of average across a number of performances. The lower the average assessment we give individual people, the lower their intelligence.

We may on occasion, however, disagree as to whether a particular action is intelligent or not. There are two reasons why we may do this. Firstly, people may disagree about the right criteria to use to judge intelligent performance. Secondly, accepting the same criteria they may disagree about the extent to which they apply to the particular performance or person concerned. Such disagreements occur with any descriptive term. It is quite possible to disagree over whether a person is short, fat or has big feet. One is more likely to disagree about whether a person is intelligent, but less likely to do so than about whether he is moral, handsome or reliable. Subjective judgement of intelligence can correlate quite highly.

b. 'Intelligence'. From such judgements where one is applying an adjective, it is possible to derive the abstract noun 'intelligence'. To anyone with any knowledge of philosophy this is dangerous ground. Abstract nouns can give one a great deal of trouble. 'What is time?', 'What is goodness?', 'What is space?' are questions of a very puzzling sort. We can avoid this sort of problem by noting that intelligence is an abstraction from intelligent people and performances. To think in concrete terms we should think in terms of the latter.

Psychologists' use

Psychologists begin with the same agreements and disagreements about intelligent people and performances as everyone else. They have no claims to authority in saying what is intelligent behaviour and what is not. What they do claim is that they can take special sorts of sample of intelligent behaviour (ie tests) and from these derive measures of intelligence. This is a large and disputed claim, which will need justifying at some length. One of the first points to be made is a statistical one. If there is such a thing as a measure of intelligence, then the different samples should give much the same result. Clearly, if different tests come up with different results then the claim fails immediately. In fact, the requirement is met. It is a safe generalisation that the general factor from one set of large and diverse tests will be close to that derived from any other. There are many such findings. These measures of intelligence are an abstraction. One can see particularly clearly in a test such as Raven's Matrices a determined attempt to exclude all learning and all features of personality such as working style, drive or perseverance. (In practice this is not always possible. People do get lower scores than they should because they are nervous, misread the instructions, are under the weather and so on. In these cases personality creeps back.)

Testing

Psychologists use tests to predict various kinds of performances which have an intellectual component.They may apply the tests to groups or to individuals.

a. Groups — The usefulness of intelligence testing of groups was particularly well established in the Second World War and they were shown to make a significant contribution towards the validity of group testing procedures.

b. The testing of individuals — This is clearly a more complex and difficult undertaking. On the assumption that the individual has obtained a true score, one can say that the result will be:

1. a poor prediction of his performance in a job or situation requiring general intellectual abilities.
2. a better prediction than any other single piece of information.

These are matters of established fact. The first is self-evident when one considers the nature of an intelligence measure. It is, as stated, a measure of intellectual performance with every element of personality eliminated. Since, obviously, success in a job, educational course, or career depends very much on such personality characteristics the value of a measure of intelligence alone is small. To make valid predictions in such circumstances one must put back estimates of such qualities as perseverance, motivation, judgement and the like. This is difficult in practice, but obvious enough in theory.

The mathematical nature of intelligence

A measure of general intelligence, which is the closest thing to a layman's notion of intelligence, is essentially a mathematical average — a sophisticated average to be sure — but nevertheless an average. An essential feature of an average is that it tells nothing about the component figures from which is is calculated. (How could anyone drown in a pond of average depth 6 inches? There is nothing here to say that it is not 10 feet deep in places.) There is no reason why a person should not be highly intelligent but inept at a specific activity such as (say) arithmetic. It is quite possible to be highly gifted at some specific intellectual task but be nevertheless generally unintelligent. And appreciating this, one can dismiss the criticism which claims there is no such thing as general intelligence but only a range of specific intelligences. The only arguments here are about utility. If one is testing for a job involving specific skills then one should use a test of specific ability. But for most managerial jobs we are looking for intellectual versatility and a general measure is more to the point. Arguments about reality and existence are not relevant to our purpose.

The question of validity

One of the most obvious questions about a test of intelligence is how it can be shown to measure this quality, and this question probably causes more confusion than any other. We are told there is no standard that one can check the measure against. Indeed, we are sometimes told with scorn that such measures match nothing but other measures of intelligence. There is a vital point here. This is that if a measure of intelligence represents a pure essence of intellect — a measure from which every non-intellectual factor has been eliminated — then there is nothing else against which it can logically be matched, for there is nothing else in our experience which consists of just an essence. So the only thing one can logically look for is agreement between different measures of intelligence. The fact that such measures do correlate highly with each other, whichever method of derivation has been used, is clearly of great significance. Otherwise there is a series of low but significant correlations with a range of achievements — occupation and socio-economic status, success within a career, examination results in many subjects and the like. There are also similar correlations with chronological age and with subjective assessments. When scorn is directed at the low value of these correlations the point is again being missed. The value of the measure is not in its precision but in its generality — the fact that it does correlate with such disparate criteria. All one can say they have in common is indeed intelligence. To put the essential point in another way, a measure of general intelligence is not of value for the precision with which it can predict any particular kind of intellectual performance, but for the versatility for which it can predict many. And the validation of the measure in turn depends on the range of correlations obtained rather than on the size in any one particular case.

Intelligence defined

The propositions advanced are by no means novel. The only surprising thing about them is that they have, some of them, sometimes been advanced by people who believed that they were attacking the legitimacy of the concept. But as they stand, they define both the layman's notion and the psychologist's general factor of intelligence with reasonable precision.

There will be those who claim that it does not go far enough in an important way. To what sort of genus does intelligence belong — is it a species of power, faculty, ability or what? To this no straightforward answer is possible. Ordinary language, unsurprisingly enough, does not have any term which is readily applicable to this kind of measurement, so that one cannot fill out the definition by placing it under such a heading. It is true that as a profession psychologists have more or less agreed to call intelligence and the like 'aptitudes'. But this is to take over this everyday term for a restricted professional use. Doing this is both reasonable and legitimate. But one cannot thereby achieve enlightenment.

There are those who would object that this account misses the central point of concern. What sort of thing is intelligence so that measurement is possible? One finds common ground here between friend and critic. The former wants to insist on the existence of some 'thing' — some non-material entity — in order to justify their procedures. The latter, pointing out that this is an impossible requirement, concludes that the concept is illegitimate. Thus S. Rose: '...intelligence is a sort of thing... that the quantity of this thing can be assessed like weighing butter in a supermarket'. In fact both parties are wrong at the point at which they agree.We are completely accustomed to taking measures without supposing that they are the names of 'things'. One obvious case is that of the 'average family'. At the moment of writing the average two parent UK family contains 1.9 children. This clearly has all the makings of an ontological scandal. What is this 0.9 of a child? Where does it exist? Does it really exist? Will it get by with 0.9 of a bed? One does not need a philosopher to comment on the dubious nature of this entity. Any hack humorist could turn out an immediate piece.

This, however, is besides the essential point, which is that such a measurement serves a useful purpose in planning goods and services. To highlight this sort of use, one can point out that if the average family contained 6 children, the three-bedroomed house and the five-seater car would not be the standard accepted articles they are today.

More to the immediate point, one might take the horsepower of a car as a useful analogy. If one knows the horsepower one knows quite a lot about its probable performance. But one does not know if the gear box is well designed, the steering reliable and one is not given any guarantee that the tank is not empty or even that the wheels are bolted on. The parallel here between a measurement of intelligence and personality factors is obvious. But no one thinks it worthwhile to ask if horsepower really exists or suggests that it is some phantom part of the engine not visible to normal inspection.

Even more profoundly, no one asks what sort of existence it enjoys when the engine is switched off. Obviously, horsepower is a useful measurement when used in the right way, with a proper understanding of what the measurement involves. Exactly the same is true of a general factor of intelligence.

III Stress

Assessors need an understanding of the way stress works for a number of reasons. Firstly, candidates are under stress in various ways and may react in uncharacteristic ways to these stresses. Secondly, successful candidates will have to cope with different kinds of stress in the job and one must be reasonably confident that they will cope with these. Thirdly, assessors may be under a stress themselves at the moment of decision, and an understanding of how this can affect decision making is necessary.

The first major problem is that the notion of stress is a narrow one and it is wholly pejorative — that is, a stressful experience is one to be avoided. The term is used naturally with others like 'fear', 'frustration', 'pressure' and so on. This is correct usage but psychologists have found it convenient to broaden the use of the term. There are a number of interconnected reasons for doing this.

The first is that stress is accompanied by certain physical changes. As laymen say, the adrenalin flows. The heart beat increases so that more oxygen circulates, red blood cells are released in greater quantities to carry this, sugar is released to power the muscles. Blood flows from the skin which goes white and from the intestines to the muscles and the brain. The bronchi in the lungs increase in size to take in more oxygen and the pupils of the eyes dilate. This is man's biological past catching up with him, preparing in the traditional terms for 'flight or fight'. The degree to which this takes place, of course, varies, but the effect does not need to be severe to be uncomfortable. Unfortunately this sort of change is not well adapted to many of the stresses of modern life. Anyone who has had a near accident in a car will appreciate that these changes occur at least several seconds later — too late to be useful. More to the present point, this is not a useful way to react to an interview or examination. The effect described, or others such as a sudden need to urinate are not helpful.

However, this is the negative side to stress. There is a positive side. This might seem surprising, but the reader might first reflect on the fact that people actively seek stress, and find it enjoyable. Skiing, diving and the whole range of sports produce the same sort of physical effect as that described, and people enjoy it. Obviously here, of course, they are using the physical resources placed at their disposal for unusual physical efforts. In a testing situation they have to control them and must remain outwardly calm. Prolonged stress of this sort which cannot be worked off in physical activity is certainly bad for people. It leads to ulcers, heart conditions and the like. But there is one physical change which is helpful in a testing situation and that is an increased supply of blood to the brain. There can be few who have not on occasion experienced feeling more alert, more quick thinking when faced with the intellectual challenge of an interview or meeting.

(There are those who wish to abandon the use of the term 'stress' in favour of 'arousal' as one that more naturally covers all the conditions described. But this is to abandon a term which is familiar for one which is not. Some readers may find it easier, however, to use the latter term.)

It has been established that a degree of stress of this sort is a positive advantage. While legend may have it that the ideal candidate is cool and composed, someone who is keyed up to the right degree is likely to give a better performance than one who is not.

But there is a point beyond which stress is a bad thing, and the candidate's performance will suffer because he has gone beyond this point. And he may do this for many reasons. Unfortunately, one of these may be that he is very keen on getting the job. Nervousness, in fact, may be an index of motivation. The candidate likely to do best is one who is not too involved in the attempt to pass. One recollects Tallyrand's advice to young diplomats 'Not too much zeal'. This applies equally to candidates. And the assessor must be alive to this issue.

Yet another complication is that candidates seldom appear obviously nervous. They are well aware of the need not to do so, and generally are able to conceal their anxieties. One seldom sees a candidate who is obviously nervous — shaky, stumbling over words and so on. Much more likely, the candidate may find his mind going blank, feel that he is answering questions at a banal level or that he has lost the point of an assessor's question.

This may well happen much more widely than one knows. There is often not much that can be done about it, but a change of topic in an interview may be a good solution.

There are other reactions to stress. A candidate may act untypically by becoming loquacious or facetious. A polite laugh by an interviewer may seem to point the candidate in the direction of an acceptable performance, and any resulting comedy will need controlling.

At this point one can hear the voice of robust common sense

asserting itself. One is not looking for nervous people. There will be many times in a person's life when he will have to face stressing situations. Making a presentation, facing stiff questioning by a senior, having to produce a paper under pressure of time and so on. There is no point in appointing people who cannot cope with these situations as a matter of routine. The assertion is valid. The implication is not. Being assessed imposes particular stresses. Follow-up research has shown that many people who were reserved or shy during selection, blossom and flourish when appointed. It is worth remembering that those who have a good idea of what the job is about are going to be less stressed than those who have only a poor understanding, but are nevertheless eager to impress. This is a significant factor at the time of selection. It is unimportant afterwards. For all these reasons apparent nervousness or self-possession during the testing procedure can be relatively poor guides to the ability to cope with stress on the job. One needs to understand why a candidate is stressed and, as already stated put greater weight on his record.

Stress abroad

Working abroad can be a stimulating and rewarding part of a person's career. But in recent years, a number of firms have become worried about the fact that some people find it stressful to the point where they are unable to work efficiently or even break down.

There are stresses peculiar to individual countries. In the Middle East ways of doing business can seem unwarrantably slow. In Japan the fact that women have no place in public or business life can put great stress on families where responsibilities have been shared. And small things — learning that the response 'yes' does not mean 'I agree' but 'I understand what you are saying', for example — can make early days there difficult. More generally, climates can be very wearing and many parts of the world are becoming increasingly dangerous to live in. In all such cases such stresses have to be balanced against the particular attractions of the country concerned.

Accommodation may be of a lower standard than the family is accustomed to. Public utilities — gas, electricity, water and refuse collection can be unreliable or non-existent. Public transport can be inadequate and getting a car maintained properly can be difficult. Dealing with an openly corrupt officialdom or a repressive government can be very upsetting to those accustomed to neither.

A manager working alone abroad or in a small office will be isolated from the network of relationships which provide stimulation and support in the home organisation. He may suffer from a lack of feedback on his own performance. If he receives criticism or is urged to achieve more, he may feel that the home organisation, is incapable of understanding the local difficulties. He can also become anxious about his promotion prospects and come to feel that he may be overlooked because of his isolated position.

Most people working abroad want to take their families with them. This is not difficult to understand. Family life not only provides one of the major satisfactions for most people; it also provides a powerful incentive for working. Families can provide powerful support for a manager, but they can also be the route by which he becomes stressed. He will have his job and his position defined for him. They may have no clearly defined role.

These days many wives want a career of their own and are not content with a domestic role. In some countries — where women are not allowed them or behind the Iron Curtain where jobs are not available to Westerners — this is simply not possible and the frustration can be keenly felt.

Sometimes it is possible for husband and wife to work for the same firm and this provides a way out. But there are problems, especially if they work at different levels in the hierarchy. However, at the moment of writing, the British Foreign Office is able to employ no less than 80 couples in missions abroad.

Otherwise wives may find themselves in a small expatriate community where their position may be determined by their husband's in the organisation. Some can rise above this situation and establish themselves as personalities in their own right. Some can accept the situation without resentment. But a wife who is insensitive to her situation or openly resentful of it, can make life difficult.

For those who willingly accept a domestic role there can be problems in dealing with unfamiliar foreign foods, equipment and services. Servants can be a bonus, but handling them does not come easily to everybody. Facilities for health care can be primitive and medical staff much less conscientious. Facilities for childbirth, in particular, can be at a veterinary level. And having to cope in a foreign language, becomes much more wearing for someone who is sick.

Children can be a source of friction. It is no longer simply accepted that they can be sent home to school and so be separated from their parents for a large part of the year. Nowadays, when bringing up children is seen as a more creative activity, parting is not so easily accepted and there are cases of valuable employees resigning for that reason alone.

Behind the Iron Curtain these pressures can be added to and exploited by the authorities. Proffered friendship from local people may have to be treated with suspicion as a possible opening move in a manoeuvre designed to compromise the person concerned or recruit them directly into espionage. Living accommodation can be bugged for such purposes and sometimes threatening situations can be deliberately manufactured, from which children may not be exempt.

Maintaining a house at home raises problems and can cause a lot of worry. Tenants can be difficult and are unlikely to look after the house in the same way as the owner. The family who found the entire interior of their house painted glossy black to serve the purposes of an obscure religious sect was unusual, but damage and shortages which the tenant refuses to remedy are common enough. Legal clauses giving possession of a house in case of an unexpected return are not always enforceable. On the other hand, not having a house can make arrival home difficult and, given the rise in prices, having to acquire a house can be very difficult.

This is, of course, a negative list which must be balanced against the advantages of living abroad. The stress experienced depends not only on the country involved, but on the individual person or family. For the right people life abroad has a stimulus and reward of its own and provided the organisation makes the proper allowances — financial and other — the experience is likely to be positively enjoyable.

At the selection stage, a number of separate factors must be considered. If the candidate is being considered for a particular country then the nature and intensity of the stresses peculiar to that country must be considered. Against this must be weighed the degree of support available from the organisation to the manager and his family. Someone going to a large established office, where advice and help from experienced colleagues is available will be less stressed than someone being sent off alone to open up a new post or market. And the degree of financial support for the move is also vital.

If on the other hand people are being recruited in the general expectation that they will work abroad at some time in their career, then their ability to resist the stresses involved must be clearly looked at.

The simplest way of avoiding problems is to ask the person concerned if he is willing to work in the country concerned or, at the selection stage whether he is willing to work abroad in general. If he is not and his wishes cannot be met, then some weighing of risks will be necessary.

The people most likely to cope with an overseas posting are those with a fundamental confidence in themselves and an acceptance of the fundamental values of their own organisation and country. Some ability at creative thinking, in order to think themselves into the way of life of the host country is an advantage. An ability at languages is an obvious asset and tests are available to test this ability.

A successfully completed tour abroad is, of course, the best recommendation, but for those without such an experience, experience of foreign parts can be explored. Nowadays many students work abroad for a time and many more travel adventurously. An interviewer who can find out what they learned from the experience, can get some useful ideas of their ability to cope.

Negative indications are, first, an obsessional temperament. Anyone who expects the details of daily life to run smoothly in accordance with habits and expectations built up at home is unlikely to cope with the inevitable petty irritations and upsets he will experience. These can come to occupy a wholly disproportionate part of his thinking.

More generally, anyone who is clearly dependent on familiar surroundings, family and friends and recreations is an uncertain risk. Equally, an assessor has to be suspicious about anyone who has never been abroad. Unless there is an obvious reason for not doing so, this must count against a candidate.

Further, the manager who simply assumes that the values of his home country should be universal and that there is no need to understand anything foreign is becoming less and less marketable. Such a figure might have had a curiosity value in former days, but in these he will come off badly when in competition with those willing to make the effort to understand the customer's way of life.

Another negative indication is that offered by a person who declares that he is better at getting on with foreigners than his own kind. If this is true he is likely to identify more with them and their interests than that of the organisation. If, as is equally likely, his belief is founded on holiday experiences, it is likely to be upset by the realities of working life abroad. And anyone who claims, for example, that he is more at home in Italy because the Italians are warmer and more sympathetic, may be revealing a need for emotional support that would make him vulnerable when separated from his familiar surroundings. More generally, someone who is not good at getting on with others or interested in learning their point of view will be at risk, as well as being bad for business.

In all this the support of the right wife can be an enormous help. (Cases of support of a working wife by a dependent husband are fairly rare, but are equally important in individual cases.) If young people are being considered in a general recruitment scheme, most will be unmarried and assessors can only work on the assumption that a sensible person will make a sensible marriage.

If, on the other hand, a manager with a family is being selected for a job abroad the situation may be more difficult. That Americans are more willing to accept wives should also be assessed. British society is opposed to overt assessment. Social occasions, whether devised for this purpose or not, are not efficient selection devices.

In this situation, the best course is probably to rely on self-selection, telling the family what it should know about the post and country concerned and what would be expected from the family in support of the manager. A check-list of points to be considered could help them to reach their own decision.

Stress on assessors

Assessors need only be normally conscientious to feel under stress when taking a decision in many cases. Aware of the consequences for the individual and the organisation, they are bound to feel under tension at times.

The behaviour of people making decisions under stress has been studied. The results can be presented simply — the decision makers tend to simplify the issues. That is they may not take all the evidence into account, but seize on particular pieces as being of overwhelming significance. They may assert that self-evidently the candidate is made of 'the right stuff'. They may elevate doubtful pieces of evidence to the status of certainty. The tendency to give weight to negative pieces of evidence has already been noted and doing this can offer an easy way out of a difficult situation.

Alternatively, there is a very strong tendency to defer to an apparently confident member of the assessing panel, despite the private reservation that their views are not well supported by the evidence.

A good assessor will reeognise these tendencies at work in himself on occasion and resist them whenever they occur.

Further Reading

These are books which give practical guidance to those engaged in assessment. The titles are largely self-explanatory.

Rosemary Stewart, *The Reality of Management*, Heinemann (1985), Pan (1986). A book that lives up to its title and should be read by anyone involved in the selection of managers.

P.E. Vernon and J. B. Parry, *Personnel Selection in the British Forces*, University of London Press (1949). Not now easy to get hold of and a bit dated, but it gives an unusually clear and concise survey of the basic problems and techniques of selection and shows in an inspiring way how limited resources were applied quickly and effectively to meet urgent wartime needs.

R. Fear, *The Evaluation Interview*, McGraw-Hill (1973). A book which covers much of the same ground as this present, but in less comprehensive terms.

B. Ungerson, *How To Write a Job Description*, IPM (1983)

Dr E. Anstey, *An Introduction to Selection Interviewing*, HMSO (1986). A clear, short and readable guide that deals largely with panel — or board — interviews.

C. Fletcher, *Face the Interview*, Unwin Paperbacks (1986). A good guide for candidates when the interviewers know their job.

Andrew Stewart and Valerie Stewart, *Tomorrow's Managers Today*, IPM (1981). A useful guide to the mechanics of some assessment centres, the reasons for using them and ways of justifying the cost.

Lewis, ed., *The Management of Expatriates*, IPM (1982). Covers the ground in general terms.

Selection is part of recruitment. The following are useful general guides to this wider activity.

P.R. Plumbley, *Recruitment and Selection*, IPM (1974) — a short guide to recruitment at all levels.

B. Ungerson, ed., *Recruitment Handbook*, Gower Press (1975)— a longer guide, which is now being re-written.

Index